Journalism and the Public

Key Concepts in Journalism

Citizen Witnessing, Stuart Allan

Objectivity in Journalism, Steven Maras

Journalism and the Public, David M. Ryfe

Reinventing Professionalism, Silvio Waisbord

Journalism and the Public

David M. Ryfe

polity

The right of David Ryfe to be identified as Author of this Work has been asserted in accordance with the UK Copyright, Designs and Patents Act 1988.

First published in 2017 by Polity Press

Polity Press
65 Bridge Street
Cambridge CB2 1UR, UK

Polity Press
350 Main Street
Malden, MA 02148, USA

ISBN-13: 978–0–7456–7160–4
ISBN-13: 978–0–7456–7161–1(pb)

A catalogue record for this book is available from the British Library.

Library of Congress Cataloging-in-Publication Data

Names: Ryfe, David, 1966- author.
Title: Journalism and the public / David M. Ryfe.
Description: Cambridge, UK ; Malden, MA : Polity, 2017. | Series: Key concepts in journalism | Includes bibliographical references and index.
Identifiers: LCCN 2016016772| ISBN 9780745671604 (hardback) | ISBN 9780745671611 (paperback) | ISBN 9781509514434 (Mobi) | ISBN 9781509514441 (Epub)
Subjects: LCSH: Journalism. | Journalism--Social aspects. | BISAC: LANGUAGE ARTS & DISCIPLINES / Journalism.
Classification: LCC PN4749 .R97 2017 | DDC 302.23--dc23 LC record available at https://lccn.loc.gov/2016016772

Typeset in 11 on 13 pt Sabon by
Servis Filmsetting Ltd, Stockport, Cheshire
Printed and bound in the UK by Clays Ltd, St Ives PLC

For further information on Polity, visit our website: politybooks.com

Contents

Contents

Figures and Tables

Figures

Table

Preface

This book began as an informal conversation. During a meeting at one conference or another, a Polity editor mentioned that the Press had begun a new series, *Key Concepts in Journalism*, and asked what I thought. I said it sounded like an excellent idea, and then I said something like, "and you can't publish such a series without a volume on journalism and the public." It is, after all, perhaps the key concept in journalism. No series would be complete without a book on the subject. She agreed, and then said, "You should write it." I quickly said yes. Later, I realized maybe I had answered too quickly. When I agreed to write the book, I had in mind a compendium of "greatest hits" on the subject, one that began with Tocqueville, grappled with Lippmann and Dewey, and made a long detour into Habermas's public sphere. It is a litany anyone acquainted with our field could recite. "I can write this book," I said to myself with some confidence.

Well, it has turned out to be the hardest piece of writing I have ever completed. I thought I knew my subject pretty well, but it turns out I was mistaken. In the past several decades, an enormous amount of work has been accomplished across a range of sub-fields. Some of this work has been published by scholars outside of journalism studies, in disciplines that rarely intersect with our own. Early on, for example, I spent six months lost in a fascinating literature on early modern English news. Published primarily by historians, in their own disciplinary journals, this literature is nonetheless extraordinarily important for understanding the history of journalism's relationship to public life. Other work has been completed by scholars of journalism, but has appeared across small subfields, like the study of Scandinavian journalism, or comparative journalism studies, or production studies, or news and technology studies. Still other work, borrowed from field theory or institutionalism, has trained a new theoretical lens on journalism. For a scholar used to burrowing into his own subfield of news production studies, reading across this work was difficult. But as I read, I began to feel that, though they wrote for different audiences about different topics, these literatures together were telling a broader story about journalism, and at the heart of this story lay some conception of the public. I knew then that writing a book on the "greatest hits" would not suffice.

It took a good long while for me to be confident that I had canvassed these literatures sufficiently. It took another length of time to piece the story together, and longer still to explain it in a way that might make sense to an interested (but not expert) reader. This last point is important, as I expect a good number of experts will read this book. As I set about my task, I realized that I had taken on a great deal of risk, namely, the risk of mischaracterizing or misrepresenting an argument, or theme, within a particular subfield. It is a risk anyone takes who attempts to write across several disciplinary subfields, which may be one reason it is not often done. As a hedge against this risk, whenever possible, I have consulted with the experts.

I run another risk as well. It is that the volume may not attend to a particular detail, concept, or argument in the way that an expert might wish I had done. An expert in field theory, for instance, may remark that I haven't done the theory justice. I should have dwelt longer on this point, or emphasized that concept. Or, an expert on a given national news system may complain that I have missed important contextual nuances about her subject. This is a more subtle risk than simply getting something wrong, and the risk is therefore more difficult to hedge against.

I worried about this dilemma for some time. Eventually, I resolved that my intention was to write for a lay audience. I wished to introduce this audience to the broad story of journalism under development in the scholarship, and to show how and why the concept of the public is vital to this story. For this reason, I chose to summarize ideas that experts might wish to unpack, and (where possible) I avoided becoming tangled in disputes they may wish to prosecute. Throughout, I provide citations for the reader interested in accessing the more dense and detailed conversations taking place in these literatures. My choices may not satisfy some experts in the various subfields. But I hope most come away from the exercise with the realization that I have not done egregious harm to their arguments., and I hope they leave with a greater appreciation for how their work contributes to the larger narrative developing in the field.

More than this, I hope that lay readers come away impressed with the centrality of the public's role in this story. If I have achieved this much, I will have met my goal.

Acknowledgments

This book took years to complete and I have accumulated many debts along the way. I want to give special thanks to the many colleagues who have read chapters and parts of chapters. They include: Chin-Chuan Lee, Judy Polumbaum, Zhongdang Pan, Michael Schudson, Daniel Hallin, and Silvio Waisbord. I want to give a special thanks to Rodney Benson, who provided much-needed feedback at several moments during this research. I also have had conversations with many people about the project. I want to thank a few of them for comments or information that have made their way into the manuscript. Among others, they include Daniel Kreiss, Peter Lunt, Rasmus Kleis Nielsen, Matthew Carlson, C. W. Anderson, Dan Berkowitz, Sue Robinson, and Seth Lewis. I also owe a debt to the anonymous reviewers for Polity, who provided helpful suggestions for making the manuscript better. A special thank you to Andrea Drugan, who put me on to the idea for this book, and Elen Griffiths at Polity, who has been extraordinarily patient with me as I slowly cobbled together the manuscript.

Introduction

Along a number of fronts, the study of journalism has made great strides in the last generation. Scholars have assessed journalism from the perspective of media systems (Hallin and Mancini, 2004) and journalistic fields (Benson, 2013). They have approached news as institutions (Cook, 1998), organizations (Ryfe, 2012), and ecosystems (Anderson, 2013). They have defined journalism as a profession (Waisbord, 2013) and as a set of role conceptions (Weaver and Willnat, 2012). They have plumbed journalism's history (Høyer and Pöttker, 2005), and compared its practice across a variety of contexts (Canel and Voltmer, 2014).

As this work mounts, the story it tells of journalism is becoming clearer. At its heart, I shall argue, stands a relatively simple idea: journalism tends to express the form of public life in which it is embedded. This is not a new idea. One finds versions of it stretching back at least to the early nineteenth century. Tocqueville's (1840/1969) famous phrase, "newspapers make associations and associations make newspapers" (p. 517), is one example of it. Carey's (1987, p. 5) declaration that the public is journalism's "god term," its "be-all and end-all, the term without which the entire enterprise fails to make sense" is a modern rendition. But it is not a simple idea. This point hasn't always been accepted or its implications understood. For decades, most observers assumed that a homogenized form of journalism was naturally predisposed to an invariant form of democratic public life. More of this kind of journalism, the thought went, equals more democracy (and vice versa). More recent scholarship suggests that this conclusion is too simple. The implications of public life for journalism are complex, dependent on a host of variables and contingencies. The need to contextualize, however, does nothing to detract from the power of the idea. There are good reasons that observers have returned to it over the centuries, and that it now animates a good deal of thinking about journalism. Perhaps no other single idea illuminates as much about the practice of journalism.

In the chapters that follow, I rely on this concept of journalism reflecting its context to tell the story of journalism that is unfolding in the literature. The drama of the story inheres in the pushing and pulling between a profession seeking greater autonomy and the social fields nearby that would shape its form and purpose. Even in Anglo-America, where for a time it enjoyed a high degree of autonomy, journalism has never gained complete control over its conditions of existence. Its boundaries always have blurred with contiguous social fields, especially the state and, depending on context, civil and political society, or the market as well. Journalism is thus always in a tussle with these other social fields. As we shall see, the story of journalism is one of contingency and probability, not of certainty, but the pushing and pulling give journalism its form and meaning.

This story has not emerged in vacuum. Rather, it has been built partly on the basis of, and partly in response to, prior thinking about journalism's relationship to the public. It seems sensible to begin there, then, with the traditional story told about this relationship.

The Tradition

That story begins in the Middle Ages. The origins of modern news writing dovetail with the rise of European monarchies. The hand-written diplomatic news sheets that circulated in Venice in the late fifteenth century were the earliest form of modern newsgathering (Stephens, 1998). By the mid-1500s, occasional newsletters, ballads, and broadsides joined these sheets, and by the early 1600s the first periodicals emerged in England, Germany, Belgium, and the Netherlands. As monarchies expanded, so did news systems. The two grew together for several reasons. First, another name for monarchy is bureaucracy, and the soldiers and bureaucrats who populated monarchical bureaucracies constituted the first sources of news (Dooley, 1999). Second, as monarchies waged the seemingly perpetual wars necessary to gain control over larger and larger territories, and centralized this control in urban centers (such as London or Paris), they also generated a new demand for news. This demand came in part from members of the aristocracy interested in news from the latest battlefield. But most of it came from the noble families of the countryside, who were keenly interested in the political goings-on in London, but too far removed from the scene to obtain this information first-hand. "You cannot imagine," one seventeenth-century English observer said at the time, "to what a disease the itch of news is grown" (quoted in Atherton, 1998). The earliest newsletters scratched this itch.

As the number of news writers increased and the amount of news multiplied, monarchies adopted two policies that further entangled them with budding news systems: regulation and subsidy.

Authorities began to make new rules about who could gather and circulate news, and under what conditions. All over Europe, for example, censorship of news was more the rule than the exception (Popkin, 1990; Roche, 1989; Todd, 1991). When they could not control the news through regulation, authorities sought to do so through taxes and requirements for "caution money," a bond or deposit against damages (Curran, 1978; Starr, 2004). When neither of these policies succeeded in stemming the growth of news, monarchies went into the business of subsidizing favored news organizations. Even as they fined, imprisoned, and taxed news producers, for instance, European authorities routinely paid writers and publishers to produce official news (Starr, 2004, p. 39).

This history is the context for the first theories of the press and its relationship to public life, which emerged around the English

Civil Wars of the 1660s. At that time, writers such as John Milton (2014) began to argue that a free press (defined as a press unimpeded by the state) was central to a more democratic public life. In this argument, journalism is seen as an outside force assisting a public—defined as a body of citizens living within a geographic territory—to gain more control over politics and policymaking. In the decades after, other thinkers such as Baruch Spinoza, Montesquieu, and Thomas Jefferson followed Milton's lead (Keane, 1991; Levy, 1985). The logic in each case was the same: to function well, democratic government required legitimacy; such legitimacy could only be obtained through transparency, that is, citizens needed to know what government was doing, and more than that have opportunities to discuss and debate these activities; in a large society, these thinkers asked, how else could this happen if not through a medium like the news? According to this logic, the press is essential because without it the whole enterprise of democracy is not possible.

What began in the seventeenth century as a radical idea was, by the nineteenth century, commonplace. Writing in the mid-nineteenth century, for instance, John Stuart Mill (1859/1978) began his classic defense of liberalism with the observation that "no argument can now be needed" as to the importance of a free press for democratic society. To Mill's way of thinking, the notion was now common sense. Tocqueville (1840/1969) offered perhaps the most famous nineteenth-century version of it when he observed: "The more equal men become, the more necessary are newspapers. We should underrate their importance if we thought they just guaranteed liberty; they maintain civilization" (pp. 517–18).

Tocqueville was not quite as sanguine about this development as one might suppose. In a democracy, he argued, power worked in a new, insidious way. "Monarchs," he wrote, "materialized oppression." By this he meant that when citizens acted out, monarchs responded with physical violence. In a democracy, Tocqueville surmised, oppression worked in a very different way. "The democratic republics of the present day," Tocqueville wrote, "have rendered [oppression] as entirely an affair of the mind" (p. 255). Majorities in democratic societies placed boundaries around personal freedom by creating a conventional wisdom about what it was appropriate to believe, say, and do. This common sense made it unnecessary to resort to violence, as people naturally curtailed their own thinking and behavior. Tocqueville coined a term for this new form of power: the "tyranny of the majority." The press was complicit in the exercise of this power. In democratic societies, he observed, newspapers were instruments of freedom, but also of oppression.

The first modern sociological studies of journalism and democracy of the twentieth century picked up on Tocqueville's pessimism. Tarde (1901/1969), for instance, warns that "the man of one book [may be] feared . . . but what is he beside the man of one newspaper" (p. 283). Far from ensuring independence and freedom, Tarde argues, newspapers tend to make their readers "homogeneous" and "pliable." That is, the news makes it easy for journalists and politicians to manipulate citizens. Writing in the same period, Tönnies (1916/2000) is, if anything, even more biting. To him, the modern press is little more than "showmanship in search of sensational news . . . exaggeration . . . exploitation." He concludes: "An honest discussion or just an honest treatment of news . . . can never be expected from newspapers" (p. 153).

Walter Lippmann (1922) consolidates these apprehensions into perhaps the most famous criticism of modern news, and of the democratic theory in which it plays such a vital role. After admitting that the press "is not so universally wicked" as many observers assume, Lippmann lists the myriad problems with the received wisdom. In the first instance, modern societies are too complex and daily news is too fragmented and ephemeral for it to convey an accurate picture of reality. Second, newspapers are too commercial and sensationalist to even attempt to paint such a picture. Third, even if newspapers wished to try, political and economic elites, who have great incentives to manage the news, would not allow them to succeed., and finally, even if publishers, journalists, policymakers, and businessmen worked together to inform the public, readers do not have the cognitive capacity to learn as much as is required to fashion informed opinions on every subject. Lippmann's conclusion: "If the newspapers . . . are to be charged with the duty of translating the whole of public life to mankind, so that every adult can arrive at an opinion on every moot topic, they fail, they are bound to fail, in any future one can conceive they will continue to fail." At best, the public is a "phantom," a fiction conjured by those in positions of political power, and promulgated by a relatively subservient press. John Dewey (1922) was so struck by Lippmann's argument he called it the "most effective indictment of democracy as currently conceived ever penned."

Strangely enough, though read widely, even today, Lippmann's indictment has had little impact on the prevailing wisdom. Through the twentieth century, common sense continued to hold that a "free press" was essential to modern democracy. In the twentieth century, Europe governments subsidized the press based precisely on this assumption. In Anglo-America, journalism was not directly subsidized. However, it did gain great symbolic power, in large part due to its reputation as a bulwark of political liberty. Certainly, journalists had little interest in dispelling the notion. When, in the early twentieth century, journalism coalesced into a more or less cohesive social field, it did so partly on the basis that the occupation played a vital role in democracy. As evidence, consider the mission statement of the Society of Professional Journalists, an organization founded in the United States in 1909: "To ensure that the concept of self-government outlined by the U.S. Constitution remains a reality into future centuries, the American people must be well informed in order to make decisions regarding their lives, and their local and national communities. It is the role of journalists to provide this information." Or this goal of the European Federation of Journalists (an organization that represents journalists throughout the European Union), "to promote the social role of journalism and the profession of journalism, particularly its contribution to democracy and freedom." Everywhere journalism professionalized, its supposed contribution to democratic public life served as an organizing principle.

In this way, a narrative about journalism and the public was born. It arose centuries ago, dispersed over time, and, by the twentieth century, became a powerful common-sense idea. Over the last decades, journalists have exported the idea globally (Chalaby,

1996), partly through the help of their governments (Siebert et al., 1956; Blanchard, 1986). The academy has played a role in its dissemination as well. Proponents of modernization theory, for instance, imagined that social development occurred in a linear direction, from traditional toward modern societies. They took the emergence of a western-style press to be a key marker of this transition (Lerner, 1958; Schramm, 1964). More generally, as Zelizer (2012) observes, "western scholarship on journalism . . . has tended to adopt the journalism/democracy nexus as a natural-ized part of understanding what journalism is for" (p. 465). Even today, a great deal of research in journalism studies is motivated by the question of whether, and the extent to which, journalism contributes to the formation of democratic publics.

The result is a particular story about journalism and the public. In this story, journalism is a relatively narrow pursuit, constrained to its coverage of formal politics. There may be other forms of journalism, among them tabloid, opinion, and entertainment jour-nalism, but they lie at the margins of the occupation. Its preferred practices are reduced to a set of elements, such as verification and balance, which orbit around the general concept of objectivity (Kovach and Rosenstiel, 2001). The notion of the public at play in this story is just as constrained, limited as it is to the citizenry that lives within the geographic borders of the state. Just as one example, the market lies outside this conception of the public, as does the state itself. With these stock characters in place, the story offers a two-dimensional plot, one in which journalism either con-tributes to empowering the public to participate in democratic life (and so plays the hero), or it does not (and so plays the villain). This story has played out in countless iterations over the centuries, and so represents a great deal of the common-sense thinking about journalism and the public.

A New Approach

In the last few decades, scholars have chipped away at this received wisdom. From one direction, historians have come to realize that journalism is not a discrete and singular object. Rather, its form and meaning has varied over time. The term itself—journalism—wasn't even invented until the 1830s, and referred specifically to the commercial news organizations then emerging in the United States, France, and the United Kingdom. Before that time, there were journalists but no journalism; there was news, but it meant something different across time and space. This point comes out especially well in a wonderful literature on seventeenth- and eighteenth-century English news production (Doty, 2008; Halasz, 1997; Peacey, 2013; Zaret, 2000). As Örnebring (2007) notes, whether packaged in pamphlets or newsletters, during this period news was not "'news' ... in the sense of reports about recent events. Instead, [it] mainly consisted of criticism ... with the intention to express and possibly influence opinion" (p. 75). Whether written by hand or printed, seventeenth-century news was rooted in oral traditions, making its form and meaning utterly different from today. In short, historians have come to see any suggestion that there is one form of journalism as woefully ahistorical.

The same thought applies to our other key term—the public. In the traditional view, the public is defined as a body of citizens who live within particular geographic borders. This is a peculiarly western, and modern, definition—but there have been others. For example, as I discuss in Chapter One, the original meaning of "the public" was the state, not a body of citizens. At various times and places, the public also has been taken to mean civil society, political society, and even economic markets. In other words, the concept of the public has multiple meanings, only one of which is the common definition today: "people who live within the borders of a nation-state." A burgeoning comparative literature on journalism illustrates this point. Think, for example, of China, which had a form of news writing centuries before the West, but which in its entire history has experienced democracy only for a few decades. In China, the public is nearly synonymous with the state. For this reason, Chinese journalism's relationship to the public is nearly untranslatable in terms of the western canon. Examples of this kind abound, leading many scholars to wonder if the canon about journalism is not only ahistorical but western-centric as well (Curran and Park, 2000; Downing, 1996).

These two thoughts together put everything into play. Not only can we not lead with fixed definitions of journalism, we cannot assume an invariant public either. Instead, we have to ask how different forms of journalism emerge within different forms of public life. Our focus is no longer on "the public" or on "journalism," but on the relationship between them. This relational approach has opened the way to rethinking journalism's connection to the public.

Siebert et al.'s *Four Theories of the Press* (1956) represents a bridge to this new approach. Theirs is one of the first studies to recognize that "the press always takes on the form and coloration of the social and political structures within which it operates" (p. 1). As they survey the landscape, they perceive four such political structures: authoritarian structures of traditional societies; libertarian structures of early modern western societies; the structure of the modern western social welfare state (and its ethos of social responsibility); and the Communist structure of the Soviet Union. As you can see, their argument anticipates the notion that journalism gains coherence relationally, in interaction with other arenas of public life. Yet, in some respects, *Four Theories* is every bit as abstract, rigid, and normative as the traditional view. For instance, it assumes that in particular societies journalism is everywhere the same. Whether an alternative weekly or a daily national newspaper, a newspaper, or a TV newscast, all news organizations in a libertarian society are colored by the same theory. Also, much as in modernization theory, there is a clear sense of historical progress within this narrative: western societies are cast as moving progressively from authoritarian theories toward a more modern (and advanced) libertarian and finally socially responsible theory of the press (Nerone, 1995). Finally, in some respects the argument merely flips the terms of the traditional argument. Where in the past journalism was taken as producing the conditions for a singular democratic public, now the public is seen as producing the conditions for a singular form of journalism. Siebert et al. perceive little *interaction* between journalism and the public.

Modern approaches retain Siebert et al.'s sense that journalism is "colored" by "the social and political structures within which it operates." However, they revise and add to it in significant ways. In Chapter One, we will consider these additions in a more substantive way, but let me briefly review three of the most important.

A good place to start is with Hallin and Mancini's (2004) three models of media systems. The authors address a similar question as Siebert et al.: why are media systems in Anglo-America and Western Europe structured so differently from each other? Like Siebert et al., they find their answer in the way that public life is structured. Where the *Four Theories* authors understand public life in terms of public philosophies (such as authoritarianism and liberalism), Hallin and Mancini define it in terms of four empirically accessible dimensions: *political parallelism*: in some societies media systems parallel the political party system and in others they do not; *professionalization*: in some societies journalism has professionalized, and in some it has not; *state intervention*: in some societies, the state has intervened strongly in the constitution of media systems, and in others it has not; and *mass markets*: in some societies a mass market for news developed and in others it did not. Variations along these dimensions, Hallin and Mancini argue, have produced different sorts of media systems. Further, since groups of nations (Scandinavia, Anglo-America, Southern Europe) tend to exhibit similar variations along these dimensions, the media systems in these societies tend to resemble one another (hence, the "three models" of media systems).

For Hallin and Mancini, public life is not *one* object (or idea, or philosophy) but many elements that interact together in time. This is to say, the relationship among the elements, and between the elements and journalism, may change over time. It is possible for social scientists to measure these elements, to detect how they interact with one another, and to trace their historical trajectory as a way of assessing how and why journalism takes the form that it does.

Hallin and Mancini go to great lengths to qualify their conclusions (see also Hallin and Mancini, 2012). They describe their models as "ideal types." They acknowledge that considerable variation exists among countries grouped together within the models. They admit that media systems are not homogeneous. Media may operate by different principles within particular societies. They note that media systems are not static., and they observe that media shape public life just as (if not as much) as public life shapes the media. The models, they write, should "not be seen as describing a set of fixed characteristics, but as identifying some of the underlying systemic relationships that help us to understand changes" within media systems over time (p. 12). Still, since its publication, their study has become a primary point of reference, as Brüggemann et al. (2014, p. 1038) put it, for an explosion of comparative work in journalism and political communication.

For all its value, however, in stimulating new thinking, the book has limits. For one thing, in confining itself to the level of media system, it doesn't follow up on the idea that different news organizations may occupy different positions in public life. For another, it doesn't explain precisely how different configurations of public life produce different outcomes for journalism. In several places, Hallin and Mancini refer vaguely to "co-existences" and "reflections" in the evolution of particular systems. In their discussion of the "Democratic-Corporatist" model, for instance, they trace the historical development of several "co-existences" between the variables (mass markets, professionalization, and political parallelism) and media system outcomes, but do not directly address the question of why these co-existences should produce this outcome rather than another. In short, they describe more than they explain. This is reasonable, given the exploratory nature of their study, but it leaves work to be done.

Some of that work has been accomplished from a different angle, that of field theory (Benson, 2013; Benson and Neveu, 2005; Willig, 2012). Field theory in the social sciences has a long lineage, stretching back to the 1930s (Mey, 1972; Martin, 2003). Among journalism scholars, however, Bourdieu's version of it has been most influential. Bourdieu's work can be quite complicated, and we will consider it in more detail in later chapters. Here, I simply wish to flag a few basic ideas to show how his ideas fill in a few of the gaps in Hallin and Mancini's analysis. The first is that, for Bourdieu, the arenas of public life identified by Hallin and Mancini—the state, political society, civil society, and the market—are not dimensions of public life so much as discrete social fields. Bourdieu (1985) defines a social field as an area of social space organized by "the set of properties active within the social universe in question" (p. 724). He calls these properties forms of capital, and they are the basis on which any particular social space is defined. This is not the place to explore why Bourdieu chose the language of economics (such as the term "capital") to describe society (see instead Bourdieu and Wacquant, 1992, pp. 118–120; Brubaker, 1985, p. 749; Lebaron, 2003). It is enough to understand that, although it may take many forms (economic, cultural, symbolic), capital organizes and orders the space within a social field by establishing symbolic oppositions and hierarchies.

As an illustration of how this happens, consider the example of the state. The state is a social field organized by its own peculiar forms of capital (Bourdieu, 1986b). Preeminent among these is the law. At its base, the law is a kind of logic, a way of apprehending and representing the world. As such, it contains preferred beliefs, norms, values, language, practices, identities, and roles. Among other things, this logic establishes symbolic oppositions. Within the state, an action may be legal or illegal (or more and less legal). This is a different opposition than, say, moral or immoral, which helps to organize the civic field, or profitable or unprofitable, which does the same for the economic field. The law also establishes grounds for distinction within the state. The more conversant one is with the logic of lawmaking (such as how to speak in legal terms, how to get a law passed), the more of this form of capital one accumulates, and, correspondingly, the more status one obtains within this field. In these ways, the law—and all its attendant values, norms, conventions, practices, behaviors, and identities—helps to organize and order the social field we refer to as the state.

Bourdieu argues that forms of social capital within social fields exercise force on actors much as physical fields (like gravitational or electromagnetic fields) exercise force on objects: by pulling and pushing actors who come within their orbit. Importantly,

Bourdieu imagines these forces as relational. In a gravitational field, the force of gravity arises in the relation of objects to one another. The larger its mass, the more force a given object applies to other objects. Similarly, actors within social fields may accrue more and less of the forms of capital peculiar to those fields, and so exercise more and less force on other actors. Within a social field, force is produced by the interaction between actors. The same is true across social fields. No social field stands alone, completely autonomous and thus immune to the influence of other social fields. Instead, social fields bump into one another, and even blur into one another. The forms of capital peculiar to each push and pull against one another. They create friction, and thus excite action.

How do these concepts help us understand the relation of public life to journalism? Well, think of journalism as a social field. Within the terms of field theory, when we say that public life "colors" journalism, we mean something like the following: arenas of public life (such as the state, civil and political society, and the market) contain distinctive forms of capital; these forms of capital consist of values and norms, identities and behaviors, practices and recipes for action; because journalism fits between the social fields that inhabit public life, they exercise more and less force on journalism and journalists, pushing and pulling them in different directions. The state pulls in one direction, the market in another, and civil society in still another direction. As Hallin and Mancini suggest, the outcome of this pushing and pulling depends on the precise configuration of the social fields, the relative strength of the forces involved, and the ability of journalism to push back.

In the English-speaking world at least, no one has taken greater advantage of these combined insights for understanding journalism than Rodney Benson (Benson, 2013; Benson and Neveu, 2005). Following Bourdieu, Benson (2006) imagines journalism as a social field structured, in the first instance, by economic capital (circulation, ad revenue, ratings) and cultural capital (the forms of knowledge, expertise, credentials, and the like valued within journalism). He then posits a role for the state, in the form of media policies, in exerting pressure on the field. Thus, on Benson's view, journalism is pushed from one direction by the state, from another by the market, and internally by a professional culture.

In a series of studies (2002, 2005, 2009, 2010, 2013), Benson uses this image to compare French and American journalism (the subject of Chapter Two in this volume). He finds that French journalism is much less oriented to the market than American journalism. Advertising expenditures are much lower in France than they are in the US, as are circulation rates, and French news companies tend to be privately owned rather than publicly traded. Further, the state has a history of strong intervention in French journalism that is virtually nonexistent in the United States. Historically, French journalism has been centralized in Paris, and emerged out of the literary and political scene of that city. It has retained these ties ever since, orienting the field more to politics and literature than in the United States.

These variations in the way that journalism is situated in public life, Benson argues, have resulted in different "logics" at work in each journalistic field, and thus in forms of news. French news tends to be more literary and polemical than American news, to represent the views of a broader range of political actors, and to structure the news in terms of debates between these actors. In contrast, American news tends to be more "fact-centered," to be more elite-driven, to be dramatized in terms of personalized narrative, and to be more politically neutral. Benson is careful to note that the two are not diametrically opposed. French and American journalism share a family resemblance. They are not identical, however. The differences between them are due to the way in which journalism is situated differently in public life. We will discuss these differences in more detail in Chapter Two.

Field theory goes a long way toward filling in the gaps between Hallin and Mancini's dimensions of public life and outcomes within journalism. In particular, its conception of social fields explains well how the various arenas of public life exert pressure on journalism. But like Hallin and Mancini's "three models" approach, field theory has shortcomings. For instance, it says little about the role of organizations in public life. In Bourdieu's imagination (1985), public life is composed of classes of people, not organizations. It also offers a vague account of how individual actors act within social fields that is not always persuasive. Bourdieu argues that the logic of social fields does not determine individual action. Rather, it shapes what he calls "habituses." In one place, he (1977) notes that were it not for its connotation of rote reproduction, he would have preferred to use the more conventional term "habit" (p. 218, n. 47). Elsewhere, he defines a habitus as a "practical sense of things," or "sense of the game" that actors acquire as they are socialized into a given field. He then links this term directly to the body, arguing (1980) that a habitus is "a state of the body" rather than a "state of mind" (p. 68). Inhabiting a habitus is a matter of bodily disposition, of implicit, largely unreflective manners and sensibilities. It "designates a way of being, a habitual state (especially of the body) and, in particular, a disposition, tendency, propensity, or inclination" (1977, p. 214). Upon entering a social field, individuals acquire its habits. They learn, in other words, to play the game. In this way, fields (or structures) create the conditions (the rules of the game) within which it is possible for individuals to act, but do not determine any particular action. In another place (1998), Bourdieu uses the term *illusio* to describe the investments individuals are required to make in the logic of a field—a "tacit [recognition] that it is worth the effort to struggle for the things that are in play in the field" (p. 78).

In the notion of habitus, Bourdieu tries to show how structures influence actions but do not determine them. Conceptually, the idea makes some sense. Much as the game of chess contains a set of rules that shape how people may act when playing the game without determining the action itself, so habituses may play the same role for the games of social fields. Empirically, however, Bourdieu's analyses tend to conclude that actors simply replicate the logic of the fields they inhabit. This has led many commentators to question why a habitus is not simply a habit, and, on Bourdieu's conception, what freedom actors actually have in resisting the habitus of the fields they inhabit (for a discussion, see Calhoun et al., 1993). How is it, in other words, that social fields supposedly endow individuals with creativity and yet in the end they nearly always reproduce the same outcomes? The dilemma arises, I think, because Bourdieu lacks a proper language for holding in place the contingency and creativity of individual action that lies at the center of his theory.

Institutional approaches help in this regard. They do so by disaggregating Bourdieu's notion of capital into two concepts: rules and resources. The interaction of these two concepts helps make clearer the connection between forms of capital and action. Several authors have noted that institutionalism shares affinities with field theory (Mohr, 2000, p. 56; Martin, 2003; Benson, 2006). In particular, like field theory, institutionalism imagines social life as being differentiated into discrete domains of activity. Unlike field theory, however, institutionalism imagines these domains as comprised of organizations. Dimaggio and Powell (1983, p. 148) articulate a principal question institutionalists ask of these fields: "Why [is] there such startling homogeneity of organizational forms and practices?" The answer, institutionalists argue, has to do with the nature of the rules and resources that structure organizational fields.

It is helpful to explain the nature of institutions, social rules, and resources via an example. Suppose I enter a newsroom. As I look around, I find editors and reporters doing this, then this, then this, in a kind of order. To the extent that "this, this, and this" represent recurring patterns of behavior, we call them institutions (March and Olsen, 1989). Institutions in this sense are nothing more than patterns of behavior stitched together as a series of rules: when producing the news, one must do this, then this, and then this. The world is prefashioned for reporters in this way (as it is for all social actors), organized into patterns of behavior (and attendant rules) that have been etched into the situations people routinely face as they circulate through social life.

Implicit within these situations are preferred roles or identities. When I take up a pattern of behavior, I also take up identities associated with that pattern. When others see me behaving like a journalist, for instance, they naturally assume that I am, in fact, a journalist. I begin to see myself in this way as well. For example, as part of an ethnographic study of newspaper newsrooms, I worked two days per week as a cub reporter (Ryfe, 2012). Early on, the behavior seemed foreign to me. I felt strange identifying myself as a reporter to potential sources. The form of writing felt odd, and I had almost no news judgment. By the end of the six months, however, the patterns began to seem familiar. As I increasingly acted like a reporter, so I felt more comfortable being a reporter. Identity and the rules of social situations arrive hand in hand.

How do these patterns come into existence? To answer this question, let's turn to another example. Imagine for a moment that it is 1939, and you have just created the first start-up technology company in Silicon Valley with your partner, William Hewlett. Such a company has never existed before in this region, and so you have a great number of questions to answer, everything from how your building will be laid out to what titles you will choose for various jobs. You aren't starting from scratch, though. There are examples from other organizations and industries. You yourself have worked for a time at General Electric and so might use your experience there as a guide. Over time, you make decisions and establish a rhythm for your workplace. Eventually, a new start-up opens down the block and hires away one of your employees. This worker brings the knowledge you've created to his new company. Instead of reinventing the wheel, so to speak, the new start-up merely mimics your practices., and then another start-up opens, and it too adopts the new practices. After all, why mess with success? Institutionalists call what is happening here "path dependency." As explained by Pierson (2000, p. 252), path dependence means that as social actors take steps down a particular path, "the relative benefits" of continuing down that path "compared with other possible options increase over time." In other words, it is more rational for an organization to adopt existing patterns of behavior than to bear the cost of inventing new ones. This suggests that over time organizations within particular fields will look more and more like one another. In other words, they will take up the same institutional patterns. This will happen partly through isomorphism (organizations copying one another), and partly through entrepreneurialism (individuals pollinating other organizations with the new ideas).

Now let's turn to the concept of resources. Patterns of behavior become institutionalized (or recur) when resources pool around them. Resources are a variation of Bourdieu's concept of capital. Sewell (1992, p. 9) defines them as human (knowledge, status) and nonhuman (money, technology) "media of power," meaning that individuals (and organizations) may accumulate them and so exercise more control over and power in the world. Resources of both kinds tend to pool around the patterns of behavior—the rules—that organize social life. Think, for instance, of objectivity as a key pattern of activity within journalism. When reporting the news, reporters adopt patterns of behavior (verifying information, balancing one perspective with another, consulting with multiple sources, and so on) that together constitute the practice of objectivity. Over time, resources have pooled around these practices and values. The more objective a reporter is, for instance, the more esteemed she will be by other journalists, and so the more status she obtains. She may also gain material capital, in the form of better assignments, better jobs, and higher pay. The more resources she accrues, the more invested she becomes in her success, the more likely she is to reproduce the rules of objectivity.

These concepts—institutions, rules, and resources—begin to unpack how Bourdieu's forms of capital motivate behavior. We have established that journalism contains preferred patterns of behavior. These patterns are linked to identity (to being a journalist, and being recognized by others as such). And, over time, resources (human and nonhuman) have pooled around them. Even so, any particular news organization or individual reporter may decide not to take up these patterns. They may decide, for instance, to lead with their passions rather than to pursue conventional, objective reporting. To the extent that they do this, however, they take a risk. Because objectivity is so central to contemporary conceptions of journalism, they risk that other journalists will no longer see them as legitimate journalists, or as journalists at all. In other words, they may lose status. They also may lose money. Advertisers may not wish to place ads in an illegitimate news organization, and traditional news organizations may not wish to hire a biased reporter. It isn't that objectivity determines actions, then; it is more correct to say that it exercises force on behavior. Individuals and organizations within the field of journalism understand objectivity as an institutionalized pattern of practices and values., and they recognize that symbolic and material benefits flow to journalists who take up these practices and values. They know what is expected of them, in other words, and what counts as legitimate and appropriate journalistic practice. Knowing this, most journalists most of the time, and most news organizations most of the time, will not take the risk of deviating from what is normal or expected, especially when rewards accrue precisely to those norms. To the extent that most reporters most of the time take up its values and practices, objectivity tends to persist as a recurring set of practices in the field.

Here then are the beginnings of a new approach. As Siebert et al. (1956) suggest, the press is colored by the political structures in which it operates. However,

- public life is not homogeneous but rather is divided into different arenas, or spheres;
- these spheres are organized by particular forms of capital, or logics, that exercise a kind of gravitational force on the individuals and organizations that enter their orbit;
- these forms of capital consist of rules and resources, which interact together to shape action within the field.

Because they focus their work on particular subfields (such as media systems, comparative analyses, organizational studies, and role perceptions), the scholars who have built the rudiments of this story have not made it plain. That is what we will do here. These three additions are a start, and we will fill in more details in the following chapters. As we will see, the value of this story lies in its rigor, flexibility, and explanatory power. It is rigorous because it identifies empirically measurable criteria. It is flexible because it opens the way to assessing various forms of journalism, practiced within and across societies., and it is powerful because it stretches across levels of analysis (individual action, institutions, and systems) to offer a cohesive, broad story of journalism, its history, current practice, and likely futures.

At its heart, this story centers on journalism's relation to public life. Carey did not know how right he was when he wrote that "the public" is a "god-term" for journalism. It turns out that public life decisively shapes journalism's form and meaning. We will spend the rest of this book teasing out what this means.

Chapters may be read in any order, but Chapter One offers more extensive definitions of key terms "the public" and "journalism," and uses the extant literature to build a model of how they are related. Subsequent chapters apply this model to particular forms of journalism, or questions related to journalism.

Chapter Two explains how journalism emerges through an exploration of two of its earliest incarnations: American and French. Further, it demonstrates how and why differences in forms of journalism may be traced back to its position in public life, and how that position may evolve over time.

Chapter Three takes up the question of whether and how our model may be applied to forms of journalism that lie outside the west. After all, framing journalism in terms of "the public" is a decidedly western idea. Is it relevant to news systems in other parts of the world? In an examination of Chinese journalism, Chapter Three suggests that it is.

Chapter Four takes up the normative tradition. As they survey the new model of its subject emerging in the field of journalism studies, Blumler and Cushion (2013) lament the passing of normative theory into obscurity. In this chapter, I show that this is not necessarily the case. In fact, imagining what journalism could or should be plays a very important role in the constitution of the field.

Chapter Five addresses perhaps the most pressing question facing the field today: what is journalism's future? New technologies have put a serious dent in the economic model on which modern journalism has been built, leading many observers to question whether the field has any future at all. In this chapter, we put our model to work to assess the impact of technology on journalism's possible futures.

Introduction

In a concluding chapter, we review the story we've told of journalism, where gaps in the story remain, and what work still needs to be done.

1

Theory

When you think of the term "the public," at least with reference to journalism, you might automatically take it to mean something like "the people," or more narrowly, "the citizenry." The public, you may say, is composed of citizens who live within specified geographic boundaries, and journalism produces news for this public. This definition is correct, but not complete. There have been at least four definitions of "the public," and each of them is an important prism through which to view journalism. Looking at definitions, journalism can be seen simply as an act of producing news. Again, this is right, but partial. It misses the fact that journalism is also a culture: anyone may be able to publish news, but not everyone is a journalist, or associates with the culture of journalism. Like conceptions of "the public," journalism has a history. It emerged in specific socioeconomic conditions and evolved differently in different places.

In the introduction to this book, I suggested that conceptions of the public and of journalism are more elastic than the conventional western narrative suggests. To see how and why this is true, it is important to get clear on these definitional issues.

Publics

In a review of the various ways in which "the public" has been defined in Western societies, Jeff Weintraub (1997) detects four alternatives. All of these definitions agree that two qualities characterize "the public": it is *shared*, and it is *visible*. But they locate the public in different social spaces, and have people doing different things in these spaces. The two oldest senses of the term derive from Latin usage (*res publica*) in the Roman Empire: the public as the state (sovereignty), and the public as the polis (citizenship). In the context of the state, the public is concerned with the administrative rule of a given territory. It is the arena in which the *rules* that govern a territory ("public policies") are made. The polis, in contrast, is the space in which citizens *discuss* those rules. In modern parlance, it is the "public sphere." As a form of self-rule, democracy combines these two definitions into one thought: citizens as sovereign. Democracy is government, as Abraham Lincoln put it, "of the people" and "for the people," but also "by the people." Put more simply, democracy is a form of government in which the people have a say in the rules that govern them. When civil society began to grow in sixteenth- and seventeenth-century Europe, a third sense of the public as civic association emerged. This is a public life defined by sociability. Think of the hubbub of city life in which strangers find themselves in constant interaction with one another. We call this arena of sociability the civic sphere. Finally, as industrialism mounted across Europe and North America in the eighteenth and nineteenth centuries, a fourth sense of the public as market took hold. This is a public of impersonal transactions ("it's not personal, it's just business").

These various definitions track with the differentiation theory of modern society first outlined by Emile Durkheim (1893/1933). The general idea of this theory is that modern social institutions have become increasingly specialized (Parsons, 1966; Luhmann, 1982; Alexander and Colomy, 1990). Political institutions have become separate from economic organizations, which have become separate from civil associations, and so on. Along the way, each of these institutional spheres develops distinctive practices, values, identities, and rules. As they differentiate further, they also become more autonomous. Organizations that exist in one sphere come to look and act more like one another than like organizations in other institutional spheres. When seen against the backdrop of differentiation theory, Weintraub's four definitions of "the public" merely describe the fragmentation of public life into distinct institutional spheres.

Before defining our four terms more precisely, I should make a qualification. In what follows, I cull definitions of the state, civil society, and so on from literatures that are vast and, in some cases, hundreds of years old. I do not pretend to do justice to the intricacy of these literatures—the turns they take or disagreements their participants take up. Instead, I merely wish to borrow from them enough to craft a definition that is accurate and useful for our purposes. When I refer to these texts, I will not pursue the many questions that one might ask; if you are interested you might start by consulting these texts. Here, we will focus on the task at hand: developing an accurate if incomplete sense of each institutional sphere within which we might situate journalism.

As Weintraub notes, the state is perhaps the oldest definition of "the public," so let's begin there. When we refer to the state, we mean primarily the apparatus of government—legislatures, legal systems, executive branches, militaries, bureaucratic departments, agencies, and bureaus—that is sovereign over a given territory (Tilly, 1992). The state may commingle with a particular religion (as in much of the Middle East), or ethnic group (which is what we mean when we say "nation-state"), but at its core the modern state is made up of governmental institutions whose purpose is to make and enforce law, or public policy, within geographic borders (Hall and Ikenberry, 1989). Both of these functions are important: making laws and policies, but then enforcing those laws and policies. This definition is simple and useful. Of course, even in its simplicity it runs several risks. For one, it risks implying that states are homogeneous, and this isn't true. Different state institutions may and often do compete with one another. No state is entirely sovereign either. Other institutions—like the United Nations or the European Union—may have something to say about how things get done in a particular state (Haldén, 2011). To make issues even murkier, the boundaries between the state and other institutional spheres are not always clear (Eliasoph, 2013). As just one example, the American military today outsources a good part of the nation's defense to private, for-profit contractors. Keeping these caveats in mind, it is still fair to say that the modern state, at bottom, is defined as the set of governing institutions responsible for public policymaking within a specified territory.

The modern concept of civil society refers to the set of institutions fitting between the family, the state, and the economy (Edwards, 2011). Many historical accounts of civil society place special emphasis on the sociability of urban centers, which grew in Europe during the sixteenth and seventeenth centuries and provided people an opportunity to meet and interact with strangers (Edwards, 2011; Seligman, 1992). Modern civic spaces are populated by voluntary associations, nonprofit groups, professional associations, churches, libraries, and more. Each of these organizational contexts is unique, but all entail a sense that people interacting within them form common bonds (beliefs and values, identities and purposes) and develop shared interests. People may enter civil society as private individuals, but as they interact with others they develop the capacity to engage one another on new, more public (shared and visible) cultural grounds.

In early modern accounts, civil society often was equated with political society (Ehrenberg, 1999). The difference between these two concepts can be confusing, so it is important to move slowly here. As we suggested above, the purpose of civil society is to develop common bonds and shared interests. But if forming collective identities and shared interests is all that a group does, we say that it remains in the sphere of civil society. It is when discussions lead people to take up collective action—that might include anything from providing aid to the poor to starting a softball team—that civic associations come to appear more like political associations., and as these collective activities come to orbit around the state, we say that civic groups begin to operate in political space, or what has come to be called "the public sphere." Thus, political society, which for our purposes we will equate with the public sphere, is the space in civil society in which people come together to form public opinions and orient state action. Political parties, interest groups, and think tanks commonly operate in political society. But almost any civic group may find itself in the public sphere. It happens, for example, when a religious group campaigns on behalf of particular reproductive policies, or when a local parent-teacher association works on behalf of a new school bond initiative. In these instances, such groups move from the activity of forming collective bonds to that of debating and deliberating and ultimately persuading public opinion.

The market is a last institutional sphere of public life, and it is easily defined: it is the sphere of economic exchange. It may seem odd to define this sphere as public. After all, isn't the economy the realm of *private* exchange and the state the arena of *public* policy? Yes and no. You must remember that markets were some of the first public spaces in which people interacted with strangers. They were therefore viewed as a place where people became civilized, that is, where individuals left behind purely private passions and behaved in recognizably public, self-interested ways (Hirschman, 1977). For this reason, it was quite common in the sixteenth and seventeenth centuries to view the market as part of civil society. As markets grew in the eighteenth and nineteenth centuries, they were seen as publics in their own right, as spaces that cultivate distinctive yet shared and visible values.

We might now ask what drives these institutional spheres to become more autonomous from one another. This question has animated a great deal of thinking among sociologists. Pierre Bourdieu's (1985) account has been influential—especially in journalism studies—so let's use his account. Bourdieu argues that the sorts of institutional spheres under discussion—that he calls "social fields"—separate from one another when they develop distinctive properties. These properties include values and beliefs, norms and rules, identities and practices. For example, in the context of the state, it is perfectly appropriate, perhaps even necessary, to compromise to achieve part of one's political goals. Cutting deals is an essential practice (or property) of public policy-making. The same is not necessarily true of political society, where the purpose is to persuade others and defend one's position rather than to make public policy. Similarly, acting in purely interested ways may be appropriate in the market but not in civil society. Within each sphere, this is to say, exist distinctive *logics*: sets of values and knowledge, norms and practices, identities and behaviors, that hang together more or less to form a cohesive system of relations (Thornton et al., 2012). We should not assume that these logics are homogeneous or without contradiction, or that actors necessarily agree on the system of relations a social logic produces. Instead, we should understand these logics as setting a foundation for interaction, and offering a set of definitions for what it is legitimate to do, and who it is normal to be, when acting in these respective fields. It is the fact that social fields contain logics that allow us to recognize when we are, say, in the political field rather than the economic field, or civil society rather than the state.

Bourdieu argues that the logics of fields are relational (1986a; Bourdieu and Wacquant, 1992). He means by this that fields are organized internally by the set of oppositions and hierarchies peculiar to a given logic. He also means to say that oppositions and hierarchies create the boundaries of social fields (the idea being that you cannot tell when you are in a social field unless you can tell when you are not). It may help to think about this relational quality of social fields as akin to setting up a camping tent. If you have ever set up such a tent, you know that you start by laying out the tent on the ground. The fabric of the tent is something like the space taken up by a social field. You then place poles through holes in the tent. I take these poles to be akin to the properties of a social field. Once this is done, two people standing on opposite ends of the tent push the poles into the ground. As the poles push against one another, the tent inflates. Social fields come into being in a similar way. They do not arise due to particular properties (or poles). Rather, they inflate when properties push *against one another* to establish oppositions and hierarchies. Like tents, social fields come into being when properties (such as values, norms, beliefs, identities, practices, and so on) interact *relationally*.

Now let me take a moment to summarize what we have accomplished so far. The institutional spheres we have defined as public are social fields. Each contains preferred forms of capital (see Table 1.1), or what we may call logics. The logic of a social field includes everything from preferred identities to conventional practices to standard norms and values. Where civic associations work

Table 1.1   **Four Institutional Spheres**

Sphere	Logic	Vocabulary
The State	Administration	Public Policy, Regulation, Management, Law
Political Society	Persuasion	Public Opinion, Debate, Discussion, Deliberation
Civil Society	Association	Association, Shared Interests, Collective Identity, Social Capital
Market	Profit	Publicity, Consumption, Commodity

to build common feeling among their members, economic organizations struggle to make money. The elements of social fields work relationally, creating oppositions and hierarchies that lend social fields a sense of order.

As Weintraub notes, the logic of each sphere is, in some basic sense, shared and visible, which makes each field a sphere of public life. Hence the common use of "public" terms in these spheres: the state is an arena of *public policy*, civil society a space of *public life*, political society the domain of *public opinion*, and the economy a sphere where *publicity* is important. Distinctive vocabularies, values, identities, and practices—what Bourdieu calls forms of capital—develop within each of these fields., and as these properties emerge and evolve, the spheres differentiate from one another, becoming more distinctive over time.

Figure 1.1 offers a generic picture of how the result of this differentiation might look. We will use versions of this picture throughout the text so let me explain what I mean by it in a bit more detail. I say the version below is "generic" because it obviously does not correspond to a real society. For instance, the three main spheres are of equal size and of course we know that is not true. Every society will contain its own configuration of public life. Within particular configurations, one sphere may be smaller or larger than the others, or, depending on the context, not exist at all.

So, the size of the spheres matters. Where they are positioned on the graph does not. Most importantly, the picture shows that the spheres blur. No institutional sphere completely separates from

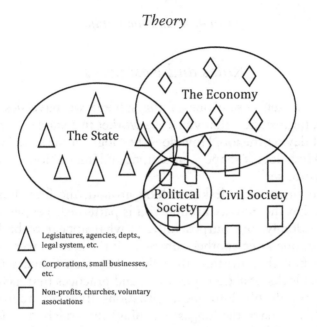

Legislatures, agencies, depts., legal system, etc.

Corporations, small businesses, etc.

Non-profits, churches, voluntary associations

Figure 1.1 Institutional Spheres of Public Life

others. This means that organizations and entire industries may straddle two or more spheres. Political parties are an obvious example of this phenomenon. In the United States, political parties have no formal role in the state (they are not mentioned in the US Constitution), yet they play an important role in public policymaking. Similarly, political consulting firms fit within political society, but as for-profit entities, also within the economy. Businesses often set up political action committees. Nonprofit groups may carry out government policy, and so on. In these blurred spaces, we expect organizations to feel the gravitational pull of the fields they overlap. We will say more about this phenomenon when we analyze specific cases.

Before considering how journalism fits into public life, let me discuss in a bit more detail the internal structure of these fields. For that, we need an understanding of two concepts: rules and resources.

Rules and Resources

Imagine yourself inside one of the spheres we have described. Suppose, for instance, that you are a worker in a state agency. It is your first day on the job. How does the "logic of the state" appear to you? How does it shape your actions and interactions, and even your sense of self?

As you sit at your desk and look around, the first thing you notice is that the activity around you is patterned. People are not acting randomly, but purposefully, in what appear to be blocks of actions, one after another, almost as if the actions were guided by *rules*: first they do this, then this, then this. Social scientists call these blocks of actions *practices*, and practices that have been etched most deeply into social situations (that are reproduced more often or have the longest standing) they refer to as *institutions*. The people around you are also acting in coordination. As they move with and around one another, their actions almost seem to be orchestrated. This implies not only that people know how to perform actions pertinent to their jobs but also they can recognize and anticipate the actions of others. They know how to act, and also how to interact with one another.

Comparatively, you feel a bit lost and overwhelmed. You have a lot of learning to do! How will you do it? Some of this learning will be formal. You may be asked to attend a seminar, during which you will be trained to perform certain actions. You may be handed a policy manual that outlines step-by-step a few of the other activities you are expected to perform. You will memorize these rules, and act accordingly, because deviation from them may bring a formal sanction. Not all, or even many, of the rules you are expected to follow are so overt. Much of the work accomplished in organizations is structured informally, and its rules are not written down. People often have a difficult time even naming them: "This is how we do things," they may say, or, "This is how it has always been done." These rules are at least as important as formal processes, but there is no systematic way of learning them. Instead, you will have to learn them as you go along. You will follow people around, watch what they do, and try to duplicate their actions. In this way, you will "learn the ropes" of your new occupation.

Informal practices are so plentiful because they fill the gaps between formal rules and the real world. The world is simply too complicated, too varied, for any set of formal rules to capture all the conditions you might face on the job. To get things done, therefore, people invent informal ways of doing things. They then pass these practices on to others informally, in conversation, or as they work together.

This is how you will learn much of what needs to be learned in your new office. You will learn by example, and then extrapolate from these examples to new situations. Wittgenstein (1958) was one of the first observers to recognize a curious consequence of this fact. If it is true that we learn most practices by performing them, then we cannot be said to "follow" rules when we act. After all, ordinarily we learn to act, not to follow rules. This raises the question: what use are rules? According to Wittgenstein, they exist less as *guides* to action than as *resources* for justifying actions that have already been taken. The rules of social action, in other words, are argumentative.

When we are out in social life, we are presented with many opportunities to make mistakes. By "mistake" I mean an action that others do not recognize as sensible or reasonable in a particular situation. On these occasions, we may be asked to justify our behavior. Why did you do this, we may be asked? It is here that rules come into play. We turn to rules to justify what we have done as a legitimate, sensible, or reasonable thing to do in this context. In the first instance, our actions are limited only by our ability to "pull them off," that is, to convince others that what we have done is an appropriate instance of the action. This lends a degree of creativity to social action that might not otherwise be visible. As an outsider, you witnessed your new co-workers acting in patterns: they did this, then this, then this. It all seemed so ordered. As you become more familiar with the organization, however, you learn that there is a high degree of improvisation in their actions. An individual may apply the same rule to different situations, and different people may apply different rules to the same situation—and they may all be right!

There are limits to what we might do, however, in any particular situation. These limits lie in community—specifically, in justifications (or rules) for action that a community is willing to accept. John Searle (1969) identified a categorical distinction between two kinds of these rules. One is a rule about how to take a particular action. An example: in chess I may move the rook up and down but not diagonally. If someone asks me why I moved my rook a particular way, I have recourse to this rule. Searle refers to such rules as "regulative." He then said that another kind of rule exists. This kind of rule is "constitutive" in that it *brings into being* or constitutes objects or situations. As an example, the rule that a duly designated authority may say "I now pronounce you man and wife" does not refer to an action associated with marriage so much as it brings marriage into being. Marriage is constituted by the expression.

I mention this distinction because the absolute limits to action lie in constitutive rules—rules about what a practice is, or is for. Or, put another way, justifications for how we perform actions ultimately lie in constitutive definitions of how things stand. As an example, imagine yourself again in the role of a new worker in that state agency. You witness a coworker scanning a very large book and typing into a computer. You ask: "Why are you consulting this book?" She responds: "I am writing a draft of a new policy and to do so I need to consult a list of current policies to ensure that there is no conflict." In other words, she justifies her actions via a regulative rule: when a public policy is written, it must be compared to a list of current policies to ensure that there is no conflict. You might be satisfied with this answer, and in reality, most of the time you would be.

Suppose, however, you asked a more basic question: "Yes," you say, "but why are you writing a policy at all?" At first, your question might elicit confusion—"What do you mean why am I writing a policy?" A more declarative statement may follow: "Because this is what I do. I am a senior policy adviser in this office., and this is what we do, we make policy." Such "is" statements represent ontological bedrock for action. Beyond such rules there is nothing to say. If you do not understand that the purpose of a state agency is to make public policy, then you lie completely outside this community. State agencies and their workers make and enforce policies, full stop. Here we see that constitutive rules (what counts as an instance of an object, behavior, process) serve as the ultimate justification for regulative rules (what we may do in relation to pre-existing objects, behaviors, processes). This insight, I believe, is crucial for understanding the practice of journalism, and I will return to it below.

Let me finish this section by making one last observation. As you insinuate yourself into your new office, you quickly learn that some roles, practices, and values are privileged. Some roles seem to have a higher status. This status may be conferred by title (such as Director of...) or material benefit (more pay). Or the status may be less formally derived. For instance, based on having worked there for decades, one of your co-workers may have a reputation for knowing everything about the office. Although her official role might not suggest it, she may be the most influential person in the office. Some practices or objects seem to be preferred as well. They may be embedded in systems or processes—things we do everyday—or material objects like computer software or policy manuals. Observing this phenomenon, social scientists conclude that *resources* pool around particular roles, norms, and behaviors (Giddens, 1984; Sewell, 2005). These resources may be symbolic (signs of status) or they may be material (money). In either case, resources appear to structure action every bit as much as rules. In particular, if resources pool around particular roles or practices, then it must be possible for people to accumulate these resources. They may acquire more skill, or loftier roles, or more money. One result is that they naturally reproduce the privileged values, behaviors, and so on, of setting. Another is that the setting becomes stratified over time (Bourdieu, 1986b). Individuals who acquire more of the resources available in this setting acquire a higher status than others.

Bourdieu in particular places a great deal of emphasis on this dynamic. When discussing the organization of social fields, Bourdieu (1984) argues that the properties (the rules and resources) of fields infuse the ambitions of the actors within them. As you become familiar with your office, for example, you quite naturally wish to be recognized as a legitimate member of the office. Recognition is linked to identity. It requires that you act in appropriate ways—as defined by the rules and resources of this context. After recognition, you may have higher ambitions. You may wish not only to be recognized but also to gain status in your office, to be seen as a great (and not only legitimate) civil servant. Accomplishing this goal requires that you accumulate more of the resources that pool around the privileged practices, roles, and so on of your office. You may learn, for instance, to write administrative rules better than others, or you may come to make more money, or do any number of a host of things to signal to others that you are a distinguished member of your office. The more of these resources you possess, the more status you gain, and the more, not coincidentally, you may be inclined to reproduce the rules and resources characteristic of your office. The more successful you are, after all, the more investment you have in your success, and the more motivated you will be to maintain the rules and resources through which you achieved your status.

This, then, is what you see when you enter your new job at a state agency. You witness people perform blocks of actions, or practices. You see them act in coordination with one another. You see them improvise and invent, justifying their behavior with appeals to rules. You see the entire enterprise anchored to constitutive definitions of how things stand. "We establish public policy, that is who we are." You see distinction. Some people have a higher status; some norms and behaviors are privileged. If you want to do well in your job, you feel the pull of the rules and resources that lend order and cohesion to the setting. You want everyone to recognize you as a legitimate member of the office, and you want to gain status. With your energies thus directed, you set out to learn how to go on, and how to achieve, in this office. In the event, you reproduce the rules and resources endemic to the setting.

All fields of public life are structured in this way, and journalism emerges and develops amid them. But wait! What precisely is journalism?

34

Journalism

The first newspaper in the United States, *Publick Occurrences* (1690), consisted of four pages—three pages of news with a last left blank so that readers could add news of their own and pass the paper on to others. To a modern reader, this seems odd. Don't reporters *produce* news and readers *read* news? For most of the history of news the answer to this question was, strangely enough, no. Until very recently there was no such thing as a "reporter," if we think of a reporter as someone hired by a newspaper and sent out into a community for the express purpose of gathering news (Schudson, 1978). People who worked in newsrooms did everything, from writing ad copy to editing stories to writing opinion pieces, but mostly they waited for the news to come to them. In fact, outside major urban areas, nineteenth-century editors were, as Schudson puts it, often "one-man bands" that performed all of these jobs themselves. Everyone else was a potential news reporter.

I start with this thought because if we assume there have always been reporters, then we might also assume that there has always been journalism. This isn't true either (Schudson, 2013). Journalism is a social invention. Before the late nineteenth century, anyone could be a journalist and so no one was a journalist; journalism, this is to say, had not yet congealed into a distinguishable practice. A few decades later, that had changed. First in the United States and England, and then in other parts of Europe, journalism emerged as a discrete activity. From about the 1920s forward, it wasn't news if journalists didn't produce it, and not just anyone could be a journalist. In some countries, journalism was written into federal law. In others, accreditation policies were put in place. Everywhere, the boundaries of journalism became clearer; standards of newsworthiness, newsgathering practices, and storytelling techniques became more widely shared, and, across much of the world, journalism came to dominate the production of news.

We will spend a good deal of time in the next chapter describing journalism's emergence. Here we focus on the elements—the resources and rules—that make journalism a distinct social field.

Let's start with this question: when journalism emerged in the late nineteenth century, what precisely was accomplished? The earliest and most common answer is that journalism became a "profession." Beginning in the 1880s, the first professional associations in journalism were created, and the first schools of journalism—mostly funded by press barons—opened on college campuses. Textbooks were written to codify journalistic practices so that they could be taught to students., and journalists—especially in urban areas—came to share a set of values and a worldview. This worldview is expressed well by one of the earliest of journalism's codes of ethics. Written by Walter Williams, the first dean of the School of Journalism at the University of Missouri, the code is called "The Journalist's Creed" (1906). It is organized as a list of beliefs, of which the most important is this: "I believe in the profession of Journalism."

Not everyone agreed that journalism was, or should be, a profession. Writing at the end of a career in journalism, Joseph and Stuart Alsop (1958) declared, "newspaper reporting is not a profession . . . it is a trade, of course" (p. 94). English journalists were especially ambivalent about viewing themselves as professionals. Still, the notion that journalism is a profession slowly took hold, so much so that it was in common use by the 1920s. As Silvio Waisbord (2013, pp. 3–4) notes, this was not out of any intention to make a normative or critical point. It simply became commonplace to refer to the occupation as a profession.

So journalism is a profession. What does that mean? Scholars have spent decades trying to define the term. Early work defined a profession in terms of characteristic *traits* (Caplow, 1954; Carr-Saunders and Wilson, 1964; Wilensky, 1964). A profession was said to contain four traits in particular: 1) a specialized body of knowledge; 2) a formal systems of instruction and training (complete with a credentialing process); 3) a code of ethics that emphasized the profession's public service function; and 4) autonomy from other professions (Bledstein, 1976; Friedson, 1986; Larson, 1977).

The obvious move is to apply this taxonomy to journalism, which is just what journalism scholars did. The result was curious. On the one hand, scholars found that journalism does not contain many of the elements we associate with a profession. For example, it does not possess a specialized body of knowledge (Allan, 2003). In fact, journalists are famous for refusing to theorize about their practice. Moreover, although journalism schools have existed for over one hundred years, in most societies journalists do not have to receive particular instruction, or be licensed to practice their craft. In the United States—where professionalism in journalism took hold earliest—it is widely understood that the First Amendment explicitly forbids government licensure. As for autonomy, journalism seems to have gained freedom from one institution (government) only to become enmeshed in another (commercialism). All of this seems to imply that journalism is not a profession.

On the other hand, scholars also found that journalism has a very strong public service ethos—as strong as most any other profession (Weaver, 1998). In recent decades, this ethos has only gotten stronger, implying that contemporary journalism is more professional than in the past (Anderson and Schudson, 2008). Further, journalism has a recognizable "news logic"— what Bourdieu calls a "form of capital"—and this logic pervades Western societies (Waisbord, 2013, p. 144). It may not amount to the sort of specialized body of knowledge found in fields such as medical science, but "news logic" is knowledge of a kind. These traits imply that journalism is a profession.

When we apply the taxonomy of professions to journalism, then, we learn that it is something of a quasi profession. This conclusion seems unsatisfying. Is journalism a profession or isn't it? A taxonomic definition of professions doesn't appear to provide a definite answer. However, we shouldn't be too demoralized by this fact. It turns out that no occupation contains all of the traits of professions. This is to say, judged by the standard taxonomy, *all* occupations are, at best, quasi professions (Abbott, 1988). A few possess specialized bodies of knowledge, a few more have credentialing policies, and many have public service missions. But none have put these traits together in a way that makes them invulnerable to external pressures—whether political, economic, or bureaucratic, and so none exists as a pure profession. This is the case even of standard professions such as medicine and law.

When sociologists recognized the deficiencies of a trait-based definition of professions, they began to look for alternatives. Out of this activity, a new tradition emerged that approached professions less in terms of traits and more in terms of *process* (Abbott, 1988, 1993). A profession, on this view, is one that develops over time in such a way that it 1) gains control over a set of work-related tasks; 2) organizes a body of knowledge around those tasks; 3) and fends off incursion from other social groups into its domain.

This process approach has several advantages. First, it places professions firmly in history. Professionalism is not a state but a developmental process that takes place under specific circumstances. Second, it allows for diversity. Some occupations may fully professionalize and others may not. Some occupations professionalize in one place and not others—or become a profession at one time and lose that status at another time., and third, it helps us to see variation *within* professions. In the same occupation, some workers may enjoy full professional status while others do not.

Only recently have journalism scholars turned to this new tradition. Waisbord (2013) in particular makes use of it to reimagine journalism. He begins by noting that the new process approach to professions has affinities with Bourdieu's field theory of society. We became acquainted with Bourdieu's work earlier in this chapter. Waisbord observes that field theory and the literature on professions come to similar conclusions about journalism. Like the process approach, field theory imagines social fields as always in motion (Schinkel and Noordegraaf, 2011). In field theory, professional knowledge becomes a resource. Individually, workers strive to accumulate more resources within their chosen fields, and collectively they struggle to gain control over tasks deemed peculiar to that field (other fields). Two dynamics are key to this process: resource accumulation and boundary maintenance. The result is a constant drive to develop, enhance, and maintain the boundaries of professional fields. The result, this is to say, is a profession that is always in flux, always pushed and pulled by outside forces, and always attempting to gain more autonomy over its domain of activity.

Waisbord concludes that it is best to view journalism more as a social field than a profession. It is a relatively bounded social space complete with its own rules and resources. No one has catalogued all the resources and rules associated with journalism (or, to my knowledge, with any social field). That said, for much of its existence, the rules and resources of journalism have included at least the five elements of Høyer's (2005) "news paradigm": stories pegged to discrete events; values of newsworthiness; the inverted pyramid style of writing; the interview; and objectivity. The dynamics of the field are driven in part by efforts to accumulate journalistic resources. For instance, a reporter may work to develop a better nose for news, or to produce more stories and produce them faster, or gain access to more sources, or exhibit more objectivity. In so doing, she may accumulate more resources within the profession, and thereby gain more status in the field (and gain more prestigious posts at better news organizations, higher pay, and so on). As a whole, reporters work together to protect journalistic forms of knowledge from encroachment by outsiders. We know that they have only been partly successful in this endeavor. Nowhere has journalism gained more than semi-autonomy from other social fields, especially the fields of politics and economics. Still, at some times and in some places, the journalistic field has been more and less intact, enough to characterize the occupation as a legitimate social field.

Part of what this means is that when publics attempt to pull journalism into their orbit, journalism sometimes has the wherewithal to push back. Examples of this process are easy to find. When the state tries to manage public opinion through the news, journalists may push back by trying to hold government actors accountable for their actions. When news organizations attempt to commercialize the news, journalists may push back in a myriad ways. Among other things, they may choose stories on the basis of different standards of newsworthiness than commercial appeal. They may write to impress one another or to win journalistic awards. And, they may refuse to learn about the business side of news.

Journalism and the Public

We are now in a position to consider the relationship between the public and journalism. How and why does the public exercise force on journalism?

A first answer is that journalism is functionally related to the publics to which it is attached. When, for instance, Alexis de Tocqueville famously writes that "newspapers make associations and associations make newspapers," he means that newspapers are a *mechanism* for bringing associations into being. Civic leaders produce news as a way of creating associations, just as policymakers support journalism as a way of managing mass opinion, businesspeople operate news organizations as a way of making money, and so on. This functional approach turns out to be quite pervasive. John Dewey views news as a way to create the "Great Community," Benedict Anderson sees newspapers as a way of fostering nationalism, and so on. It is common because it is so intuitive. People have a need to hail, organize, maintain, and facilitate publics (whether they are within the state, the market, civil society, or political society). Journalism is one way they accomplish these tasks. To the extent that this is true, the rules of journalism obviously will be strongly shaped by the logics of the other social fields its serves.

The nineteenth-century American party press is one example of how this works. From roughly 1830 to 1890, the number of American newspapers grew exponentially, and most were associated, either formally or informally, with political parties. Parties sometimes owned newspapers outright. More often, they subsidized newspapers by giving their owners jobs (as, for instance, postmasters) and providing them a ready supply of subscribers. In exchange, newspapers simply carried out the party's business (McGerr, 1986). They celebrated party events, informed party members of the party platform, castigated the opposing party, and so on. In doing these things, newspapers showed themselves to be functionally bolted onto the party system.

As I say, this functional approach is the most common way of thinking about the relationship of the public to journalism. If associations in public life need journalism, it stands to reason that the journalism they produce will express the rules of the field. A commercial news organization will express the properties of the market, a state organ will express properties endemic to the state, and so on.

James Carey (1989) and Michael Schudson (1998) have perhaps been most insistent that publics also shape journalism in a second way. Journalism, to their mind, is not simply a mechanism; it is a form of culture. As such, it cannot be reduced to a function of something else. It is a thing in itself, with its own logic and rules. This is the sense of Carey's point that of all the things the news does, one of the most important is that it "portrays" the world as it "at root is" (1989, pp. 20–1), an observation that is similar to Hegel's formulation that news orients us "to that which the world is" (quoted in Buck-Morss, 2000). In representing an association, news not only serves as a guide for action in that venue; it tells us what an association is. Schudson (1998) means to say something similar when he writes that news conventions "reinforce certain assumptions about [our] political world" (p. 55). The point is that the news is not only a tool for bringing publics into being. It is also a way of expressing the constitutive rules of public life—what public life, at bottom, *is*. This is a powerful way of understanding journalism's relationship to publics: the culture of journalism is enmeshed, more and less, in the constitutive commitments of contiguous social fields. This idea is especially powerful in situations—as is common today—when journalism is not contained within a single publics but stretches across two or more.

Schudson's work on the narrative form of the nineteenth-century American party press shows how news as culture is enmeshed in other social fields. As I said above, the party press can be seen as a mechanism for promoting political parties. At the same time, Schudson argues, the party press also expressed an underlying reality of party life, namely, that affiliation with the party was not only the way things were, it was also the way things ought to be (Schudson, 1998). Parties were a primary engine for producing and reproducing a culture of association. How did newspapers express this culture? They did so by adopting such practices as the use of personal pronouns ("I," "me," "we"), focusing their reports on crowds rather than leaders, and, narrating events in chronological form (Schudson, 1998). In such practices, news expressed a key value of public life: that people do and should associate themselves with larger political groups.

Ryfe (2006) extends this point to note that abolitionist and suffragist newspapers—both of which lay outside of party politics—used personal pronouns in their stories too, focused on crowds more than leaders, allowed many voices in their coverage, and so on. Associationalism, it appears, was not only a mechanism for achieving party goals; it was also a cultural value that extended across American public culture. Given this fact, it should not be surprising that even newspapers outside the party structure incorporated this value into the news. In so doing, they showed themselves to be participants in culture and not merely members of particular groups.

There is a looming question here. It has to do with how a dominant culture of public life forms. How did it come to pass, for instance, that associationalism dominated so much of American public life in the mid-nineteenth century? There is no easy answer to this question. Raymond Williams (1976, p. 121) suggests that at any moment in time, a society may have a tendency to privilege certain strands of culture (of beliefs, practices, ideas, and so on). These strands become dominant because they are pervasive, meaning that they are widely shared across the various arenas of public life. Their dominance, Williams hastens to add, is not static or total. Rather, dominant strands of culture are always in some degree of conflict with residual and emergent strands of culture. Their interaction is dynamic. It leads people who prefer the dominant culture to attempt to incorporate deviant cultural strands, and it leads advocates of residual and emergent strands to oppose the dominant culture. For our purposes, this framework seems sensible. When we refer, then, to "the culture of public life," we mean the state of play at a given moment in time between dominant, residual, and emergent cultural forms., and when we say that journalism expresses public life, we mean that it makes manifest these cultural strands and the relation between them in another medium—that is, the news.

Using our concepts of rules and resources, we can say more about just how journalism comes to express public life. Suppose for a moment you are a journalist writing a story about an event. You have reported the event, and now you must sit down and weave a story together out of the information you have collected. How will you do this? Ordinarily, you will stitch together the information you have collected—that is, you will create culture—in ways that are *recognizable* to your audiences, or, put another way, in ways that are culturally available to audiences (Lamont and Thévenot 2000). Put simply, you will tell stories that make sense to your audience. After all, to do otherwise risks making the news unrecognizable to the very people who will consume it. In this way, journalists embed within their stories institutionalized cultural assumptions (that is, rules) of the public life in which they act. As they do so, they lend greater symbolic weight (that is, add resources) to precisely these assumptions, and so help to reproduce the dominant culture. An easy example of this process is the ethnocentrism of most national news media (e.g., Gans, 1978). American news media portray the world through the prism of typically American values just as Brazilian journalists convey the news in conventionally Brazilian ways. In so doing, they both express and reproduce the cultural assumptions of the societies in which they operate. For journalists to do otherwise risks making the news unrecognizable to the very people who journalists wish to reach. The requirement that news be recognizable binds news as a form of culture to the culture of public life.

But journalism never lies completely within one sphere of public life. Rather, it is pulled across various spheres of public life. Journalism in the United States, for instance, is pulled in one direction by commercialism, in another direction by the state, and in still another direction by the profession itself. In this situation, how can we say that journalism expresses anything like a coherent public life?

Here, we may return to the relationship between regulative and constitutive rules. The constitutive rules of journalism—what it is and what it is for—are strongly shaped by the broader commitments of the publics in which journalism is embedded. In a market, the purpose of journalism is to make money, while in civil society its purpose is to promote association, and so on. Notice that these purposes lie in the background as a kind of common sense about journalism. As such, they open a space for action. They tell us "we are here to make money," or, "we are here to promote affiliation and belonging." But they say nothing about how to achieve these purposes, or how to practice journalism.

Regulative rules—the practices of journalism—arise as all the things journalists do to achieve these constitutive purposes. It is important that journalists learn these practices by, well, practicing. Whether that practice takes place in a newsroom or a classroom, journalists learn to do "the right thing" in the right situations. In part, this means that the rules for how to do journalism do not precede its practice—journalists do not "follow rules" when they produce news. Rather, they simply produce the news. Regulative rules only come into play when journalists are asked to *justify* their practices. Why did you, reporter, choose this story rather than that one? Why did you write the lead this way rather than that? Journalists are asked these questions every day. Strangely enough, they turn to rules for how to practice journalism *after the fact*, and use these rules as justifications for things they have already done.

We might now add that journalists may turn to different rules to justify different practices, and the same rule to justify the same practice. This means that there are aesthetic and political dimensions to news production. Journalists' success in justifying their actions depends upon their ability to convince others that what they wish to do (or have done) is appropriate and legitimate. Some of this ability is performative: that is, some journalists are simply better at arguing their case., and some of it is political, in the sense that some journalists have accrued more cultural capital within the field of journalism, and their status itself gives them more leeway.

What are the limits of this exercise? Well, they lie at the boundaries of community. That is, they lie at the boundaries of what a journalist can do and still be recognized by others as practicing journalism. This is another way of saying that the practice of journalism finds its ultimate justification in underlying constitutive purposes.

As an illustration, consider the practice of balance. Every American reporter knows she ought to produce stories that balance one point of view with another. This is a standard practice (or regulative rule) of the profession. Suppose we were to press her on this. Why balance points of view? She might respond that it is important to offer competing perspectives. If asked why this is the case, she might say that readers ought to be allowed to make up their own minds about the issues. If we continue to press her, she will finally end up saying that readers need to be informed about the issues so that they can make up their own minds. She has come to a kind of ontological bedrock: journalism, at bottom, *is* the act of informing citizens. Here, the practice of balance finds its final justification in a constitutive commitment—namely, that journalism's purpose is to inform.

If we pressed our reporter still further, to ask why journalism ought to inform citizens, she might say that journalism should do this so that citizens can develop informed opinions., and if we ask about informed opinions she may say that citizens need to develop such opinions so that policymaking can be guided by an educated public opinion. We have now come full circle, back to the relation of journalism to public life. Journalism's constitutive purposes are rooted in the broader cultural commitments of public life (Alexander, 1981). In this case, a conventional practice of journalism is wedded to a theory of democracy: that policymaking ought to be guided by informed public judgment. Connecting these dots, we see that a practice of journalism, in this case balance, is ultimately justified in terms of constitutive commitments (or the dominant cultural strands) of the public life to which it is attached.

In theory, this leaves us with an image of journalism as a deeply unstable social field. After all, if different practices can be justified in terms of different purposes, this doesn't seem to lend much cohesion to the field. In practice, however, journalists tend to develop routine justifications for their work. These justifications arise on the fly, in practice, as journalists are challenged to explain what they do. As they build up a repertoire of these

responses, journalists produce and reproduce particular relationships between practice and purpose. Journalism gains stability
in these relationships., and as the culture of journalism becomes
more stable, its relationship to public life becomes (more and less)
settled too.

The culture of news, then, is enmeshed in the culture of public
life. That said, the precise relationship of journalism to public life
depends on many things: it depends on the configuration of public
life and its constitutive commitments. It depends on the relative
autonomy of journalism from the publics in which it is embedded.,
and it depends on the range of arguments journalists can make and
still be recognized as doing journalism. In the abstract, we will find
no firm answers to the question of the relation of journalism to
public life. However, the tools we have developed in this chapter
(our four definitions of the public, the notion of journalism as a
social field, the process of recognition, constitutive and regulative rules, the role of justification in the production of journalistic
culture) allow us to find those answers in the circumstances of
specific cases.

In Chapters Two and Three, we learn how this is done!

2

Emergence

In Chapter One, we laid out a set of tools for thinking about journalism in relation to the public, but we did so in an abstract way. The thrust of the argument is that journalism may be arrayed across four distinct arenas of public life. Each of these arenas contains a set of rules and resources, what I have called a logic. This logic pushes and pulls organizations in their orbit. As a public institution, journalism inflates as news organizations come to respond in similar ways to this pushing and pulling. A variety of professional practices and values have migrated around the globe, lending journalism practices everywhere a family resemblance, but these instances of journalism are not precisely the same anywhere—there is no single example that is the model. Because public life is configured differently in different societies, the journalistic field gains a shape peculiar to local circumstances.

As I say, this is a lot of theory. To grasp its implications, we need to put the tools to use. In this chapter, we do so in the context of a famous comparison, that between France and the United States. Observers have been comparing these societies since Alexis de Tocqueville (1840/1969) traipsed across the United States in the 1820s. The attraction is obvious. France and the US had the first democratic revolutions of the modern age. Ever since, the two countries have been taken as archetypal examples of modern democratic societies. Yet in each nation democracy has unfolded very differently. Most obviously, markets loom about as large in the American context as the state does in France. Such differences have made for dissimilar configurations of public life. Observers use these similarities and differences to think through how democratic societies organized differently respond to a variety of issues, from poverty to immigration, race to cultural production (see Lamont and Thévenot, 2000, p. 18, n. 3).

Scholars of journalism have contributed their fair share to this conversation (Alexander, 1981; Albert, 2004; Benson, 2013; Boudana, 2010; Chalaby, 1996; Neveu, 2009). As you might suspect, they have discovered that French and American journalism share many commonalities. News organizations, for instance, are structured in similar ways. Journalists in each country embrace many of the same values (Boudana, 2010; McMane, 1993). They also use many of the same practices (sourcing, beat reporting) and forms of writing to present the news. Scholars have been as impressed with the differences as the similarities between the two, however. Generally, they have found that American journalism is more information- and fact-oriented, while French journalism is more debate- and literary-oriented (Benson, 2002, 2005; Benson and Saguy, 2005; Chalaby, 1996). These differences are not absolute. It is not as if French journalists, for instance, do not also gather facts, or American journalists have no literary aspirations. But the dissimilarities in the form of news are real.

We can trace these differences back to the location of the journalistic field in the public life of these societies. In our terms, the similarities of the two fields are due to the fact that they emerge, as does journalism across the West, primarily in a nexus between the state, political society, and the market. As such, news organizations across the West are presented with relatively similar opportunities and constraints. These opportunities and constraints, however, are not precisely the same. In France, for instance, the state and political society have exercised great force on journalism, while in the US markets weigh more heavily. These divergences push and pull journalism in slightly different directions. The results can be seen in the norms, practices, and roles journalists take up in the two societies, and ultimately in the form of news.

This is the broad story we will tell. Along the way, we will fill in many details. By the end, we will have learned something useful and interesting about the role the public plays in the formation of journalistic fields., and we will have gained a greater appreciation for the diversity of ways in which it may play this role.

Early Cases

Friction plays a crucial role in the formation of social fields. Inflation, after all, requires heat (think of bread rising in an oven), and heat requires friction. For journalism, absent the state's willingness to grant it breathing room, there is no friction, and without friction, the field cannot inflate. Not surprisingly then, journalism emerged first in the United States in the late nineteenth century, and a bit later in the UK, the two places where the state first gave journalism a bit of space to grow. Before this happened, journalists lived itinerant, fragile lives (think of the seventeenth-century Grub Street in England, and its parallel in France), or their work was considered part of another activity, like party politics or literature, business or state administration. There was no *journalism*—a more or less autonomous occupational field with its own rules and resources.

In this section, I tell the story of journalism's emergence, first in the context of the United States and later in the context of France. Like all such stories, it begins with the state.

One might think that the First Amendment to its Constitution settled the matter of state interference with the press in the United States. After all, the amendment declares, "The Congress shall make no law . . . abridging the freedom of speech, or of the press." Yet, beyond separating the new country from the English common law tradition, it was not clear what the framers intended by this phrasing (Levy, 1985). This ambiguity allowed great room for interpretation. It may surprise you to learn that, for much of their history, Americans have interpreted the amendment to mean that the press had, and should have, *limited* freedom. Through the nineteenth century, it was not unusual for state officials to censor the local press. This is especially the case for publications that represented the views of unpopular groups, such as abolitionists, or labor unions, or women suffragists, which were subjected to especially strong censorship. But it was also true, more or less, for any newspaper that ran afoul of local sensibilities.

Political parties represented another kind of constraint on newspapers. By the mid-nineteenth century, the United States contained vastly more newspapers than any other country in the world (Starr, 2004). More than 80 percent of these publications were directly or indirectly tied to political parties (Kaplan, 2002; McGerr, 1986). It is true that the penny press—commercial news-papers that emerged in the larger cities along the Eastern seaboard in the 1830s—were less entangled with political parties than party papers (Baldasty, 1992). But as Schudson (1998, p. 120) observes, while these papers often "preached independence," they "prac-ticed partisanship." Even the growing commercial press, in other words, was entangled with the parties.

What did this mean? It meant, among other things, that newspa-per editors were often leaders of party organizations and even ran for office (McGerr, 1986). It meant that newspapers were either directly owned by the parties or, more often, indirectly subsidized through subscriptions by party members. It meant that when it came to political news, newspapers generally adopted a party line and defended it against the opposing side. It meant that much of the information published in newspapers came from party events and party leaders. It meant, finally, that news writing was widely understood as an appendage of party politics, and through them, the state. As I say, these characteristics were strongest among explicitly party-affiliated newspapers. But the culture of partisan-ship influenced even the most commercial of newspapers, linking them to parties in a way that forestalled the growth of journalism.

Strangely enough, the five elements of Høyer's (2005) news paradigm—stories pegged to discrete events, values of newswor-thiness (e.g., timeliness, immediacy, impact, proximity, relevance, and so on), the inverted-pyramid style of writing, the interview, and objectivity—were all introduced in the nineteenth-century United States. The first interviews were done in the 1830s and became a common practice in American journalism by the 1860s (Stephens, 1988; Schudson, 1996). Though the term "objectivity" was not in wide use until the 1920s, it was not unusual for journalists to proclaim their neutrality and independence seventy years before (Chalaby, 1996). News values such as timeliness and impact were already apparent in the human-interest stories of early nineteenth-century penny papers (Schudson, 1978). The inverted-pyramid style of writing, which Pöttker (2005) defines as the lead + body principle, in which a lead paragraph answers the 5–W questions, was in use during the American civil war and commonplace by the 1880s.

However, these elements did not jell together into a relatively cohesive journalistic field until the next century. We might ask why it took so long for this process to happen, but a better question is why it happened at all. As we have learned, for much of their existence, American newspapers remained part and parcel of party politics. How and why did journalism gain a measure of autonomy? And why did this happen first in the United States and not elsewhere?

The short answer is that, in the last part of the nineteenth century, American public life changed, and these changes opened a social space for journalism to occupy.

The long answer begins with commercialization. Through the nineteenth century, urbanization, increased literacy rates, a growing economy, and new technologies of production and distribution (the rotary printing press, the telegraph) created a larger market for news. Entrepreneurs rushed into this market, and as they did their actions lent journalism more cohesion. For instance, businesspeople quickly realized that fickle and inattentive audiences demanded *greater and greater quantities* of news, as did the growing number of companies that wished to place ads on news pages (Baldasty, 1992). So newspapers could no longer wait for the news to come to them. Instead, they had to hire more reporters, and more reporters meant more opportunities for a culture of journalism to grow.

As the number of newspapers increased, the competition for audience attention, especially in the larger cities, intensified as well. Part of what this meant is that newspaper owners also needed news *faster* (Wiener and Hampton, 2007). Increased speed required that reporters have greater autonomy from publishers and editors. It also meant that they had to make quicker, more automatic judgments about the newsworthiness of events. This is one source of journalism's vaunted sense of newsworthiness. Reporters also had to develop more efficient and standardized methods for gathering and reporting news. So not only did they begin to develop a shared culture, they also began to create shared practices. As news became a commodity, it also became more *fungible*. Stories reported and written by one reporter came to look similar to those reported and written by any reporter. These shared practices lent news columns uniformity and predictability. They also allowed stories reported in one place to be published in another. News, in a word, became *industrialized*.

Finally, objectivity in the news derives in part from commercialism (Schudson, 2001). The demand that reporters remain objective served the purpose of de-radicalizing them, thus ensuring that journalists' politics did not get in the way of their employer's business interests (Schiller, 1981). Objectivity also distinguished the news from other forms of mass entertainment that were emerging at the same time (hence, *The New York Times* motto, "All the News That's Fit to Print"). It allowed newspapers to appeal to a mass audience rather than a partisan audience (Emery et al., 1996), and finally, objectivity allowed news managers a measure of control over reporters (Breed, 1955). In all of these ways, objectivity—a cardinal value of journalism—has roots in the business interests of news owners.

If the long answer to the birth of journalism begins with commercialism, the story does not end there. In the largest American cities, highly commercial, mass-market newspapers existed by the 1870s and 1880s, yet journalism did not fully appear until the 1920s. What else was needed?

Aside from commercialism, a transformation of government was perhaps the most important impetus for the rise of modern journalism (e.g., Kaplan, 2002; Ryfe, 2006; Schudson, 1998). Journalists had been striving for greater autonomy from the state for hundreds of years (e.g., Levy, 1985). The First Amendment guaranteed American journalists a greater degree of autonomy than anywhere in Europe. But as in Europe, these same journalists remained yoked to political parties through the end of the nineteenth century. Schudson (2005, p. 98) lists the changes that happened rapidly thereafter: "the adoption of the Australian ballot, civil-service reform, corrupt practices acts, voter registration laws, the initiative and referendum, the popular primary, the direct election of senators, and non-partisan municipal elections." These changes made the state overtly hostile to political parties. For example, with the onset of civil service reform, the parties could no longer use government jobs to stimulate party loyalty., and the introduction of the Australian ballot (or secret ballot) meant that parties could no longer be sure their members voted in prescribed ways. As a result of these changes, the power of parties over the political process, and over journalism, waned.

Journalists were primed to seize the opportunity that lay before them. Simply put, journalists wanted to professionalize. The extent of their motivation is a third ingredient for the rise of modern journalism. Even though commercialism and government reforms opened the way toward greater cohesion in journalism, journalists did not have to grasp the opportunity. What is important is that they fervently wished to do so. Why? Partly, it came from centuries of low pay and even lower status (Hardt and Brennen, 1995). They simply wanted better lives, which they thought might be gained by greater organization of their discipline. It also came as part of the great sweep of professionalization then taking place in American society. As Nathan Hatch (1988, p. 3) notes, "the concept of *the professions* for a whole range of occupations has arisen historically only in the Anglo-American world" (italics in original). Unlike in most of Europe, where the state controlled so much of public life, in the United States (and to a lesser extent, in England) occupations were made to scramble for resources and prestige. Already in the 1830s and 1840s, occupations such as law and medicine began to organize, codify, and patrol the boundaries of newly configured professions. By the end of the nineteenth century, many occupations were struggling for a similar status, journalism among them.

One way to think about journalism's emergence in the US is

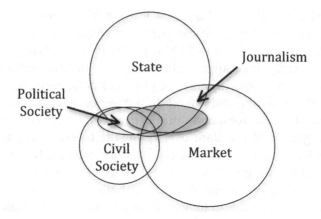

Figure 2.1 The Journalistic Field in the United States

to see that it inflated as a social field in the friction created by heightened commercialism, changes in the state's approach to journalism, and professionalism (see Figure 2.1). Each of these processes was important, but the *relationship* between them was vital. Journalism would not have emerged as a social field without the pushing and pulling among the forces of commercialism, professionalism, and state policy. Return, for a moment, to the tent metaphor I introduced in Chapter One. The state, the market, and the profession represent the poles of the journalistic field. As these poles began to push and pull against one another, journalism began to inflate as a social field.

The French Counter-Example

For a brief moment after the French Revolution in 1789, it appeared that French journalism might follow the same path— only one hundred years earlier. For two centuries before, as in most of Europe, the French monarchy had kept very tight control over journalists. The monarchy banned British and other foreign papers from entering France, and publishers were made to acquire a royal privilege to print or write. In fact, the government went so far as to assign particular censors to specific publications (e.g.,

Todd, 1991) to ensure that nothing untoward was published. Punishment for violating censorship rules was also severe. Daniel Roche (1989) reports that in the eighteenth century, nearly 20 percent of prisoners in the Bastille were journalists (p. 23).

Still, underneath this censorship system a culture of commercially oriented literary journalism began to grow (Censer, 1994; Censer and Popkin, 1987; Darnton, 1985). Though poorly paid, French writers gained a measure of prestige, and the occupation of journalist slowly became a way for ambitious young men to make their way into the society of letters (literature and the academy). The pamphlets they produced were officially illegal (Popkin, 1990), but because they avoided discussions of politics they generally were left unmolested by government officials. While the audience for these publications was limited to the bourgeoisie and aristocracy (Censer and Popkin, 1987), in its national postal system France built one of the most advanced distribution systems for news in the world (Todd, 1991, p. 28). All of this meant that at the onset of revolution, France was equipped with a distribution system, a commercially (if not politically) oriented press, and a ready stable of journalists.

As the revolution swept aside longstanding constraints, journalism exploded. The country, W. R. Murray (1991) writes, went from having a "virtually non-existent political press before 1789 [to the] most advanced political press in the world" (p. 161). Following the Americans' lead, the revolutionists proclaimed as their eleventh "right of man" that "the free communication of ideas and opinions is one of the most precious of the rights of man. Every citizen may, accordingly, speak, write, and print with freedom." Under this protection, more than 130 new political newspapers entered the French market in 1789 (Gough, 1988, p. 21), another 300 emerged in Paris alone in 1791, and another 300 emerged in 1792. French journalists were the first to invent new on-the-scene styles for reporting that gave readers a visceral feel for political events as they unfolded in real time (Censer, 1994: p. 29). They were also the first to invoke a new ideal, namely, that journalism represented "the public" (Baker, 1990). As they took up and defended political positions, journalists passionately engaged this public. In so doing, Popkin (1990) writes, "the press [became] the vehicle by which politics was made public and therefore legitimate, and concretely the newspapers provided a babble of voices" (p. 5).

By the early 1790s the French had the largest and most modern press corps in the world. Yet journalism never fully blossomed in France, at least not until the twentieth century, and has never professionalized to the same extent as in the US. The story of why this is the case is nearly the reverse of the narrative we just told.

In the first instance, the state never stopped interfering with the French press. To be sure, through the nineteenth century the state continually reaffirmed the principle of the freedom of the press. Yet at every opportunity it practiced censorship (Kuhn, 1995, p. 51). The nineteenth century was a tumultuous period in French politics. Napoleon took power in 1804, only to be supplanted by the return of monarchy in 1824. The July Revolution of 1830 ended the monarchical period once and for all, and led to the establishment of the Second Republic in 1848. It did not, however, end the age of empire, which continued with the ascension of Napoleon III in 1852. France finally became democratic with the rise of the Third Republic in 1870. In the periods of turmoil between these governments, journalism gained ground. For instance, journalists were instrumental in instigating the July Revolution of 1830. But once in power, every government quickly imposed new press controls.

The press law of 1881 seemed to end this pattern. Passed during the Third Republic, this law, as Kuhn (1995) describes it, "abolished 42 former laws containing 325 separate clauses, which had been passed over 75 years by ten different regimes" (p. 52). In place of this dense cluster of regulations, the Law on the Liberty of the Press, as it was formally called, declared, "Printing and publishing are free." With this pronouncement, a so-called golden age for French journalism ensued, lasting until the onset of World War One. In this period, markets for news grew. According to Albert (2004, pp. 24–5), at the beginning of the war, France had a circulation rate of 244 newspapers sold per 1,000 residents, a rate comparable to that in the US. American-style reporting also migrated to Paris, as owners of commercial news organizations sought to capitalize on their newly won freedom to publish. At the time, it looked as if French journalism might emerge in tandem with the profession in the US and the UK.

Yet again, France did not follow the American and British examples. For one thing, while a market for news developed in France, it was never very large (Hallin and Mancini, 2004, p. 92). This was mostly due to the fact that the French advertising market was only about one-sixth the size of the American market, meaning that French industrialists never had a great incentive to invest much money in the enterprise. Instead, most French newspapers were owned by industrial cartels. These combinations used newspapers to increase their political influence rather than their wealth (Chalaby, 1997). Commercialization, in other words, never quite took hold in France the way it did in the US and UK.

Moreover, although the state formally pronounced the press free, in practice it continued a long tradition of meddling. Corruption, for instance, remained rampant. Chalaby (1996, pp. 321–2) notes that the French government continued a practice of paying for news coverage that stretched back to the Ancien Régime. French journalists even took bribes from foreign governments. More broadly, Baker (1990) argues, the French people tended to view the "public" as an abstract, unified entity. This meant that once the state divined the "public's interest," it could brook no disagreement. Given the generally unruly—and violent—competition among political groups for political control, French journalists had little opportunity to position themselves as neutral arbiters of public information. In the US, where political conflict was more muted, American journalists could imagine their work as quasi-scientific. In contrast, French journalists were forced to take a side and defend a political position. As Chalaby (1996) observes, "within this political context, journalists could not but be the instrument of political cliques and factions" (p. 319). Through the golden age of French journalism, then, newspapers remained strongly aligned with political parties.

Finally, unlike their American counterparts, French journalists had no great interest in professionalizing. Instead, they retained deep investments in the literary world. For the French, journalism was a "provisional occupation," as Chalaby (1996, p. 314) describes it, and their greatest ambitions lay in the literary field. Newspapers, Ortega and Humanes (2000, p. 125) write of France and similar Mediterranean countries, "valued more highly writers, politicians and intellectuals," and journalism was a "secondary occupation, poorly paid and to which one aspired often as a springboard to a career in politics" (quoted in Hallin and Mancini, 2004, p. 110). For this reason, French journalists remained only weakly professionalized through the first half of the twentieth century. This did not mean, as Hallin and Mancini (2004, p. 110) note, that French journalists were less educated or in some way inferior to their American counterparts. Rather, it means that they simply had little desire to separate their work from political or literary fields.

We might say that journalism in France failed to inflate. It failed to inflate mostly because the French state never opened a space for it to do so but also because the market for news was much smaller. It is also the case that, as compared to the US, French civil/political society was more diverse and tumultuous (see Figure 2.2). (This implies, by the way, that while friction is necessary for journalism to inflate, too much friction can have the opposite effect.) French journalists found a more natural home in places

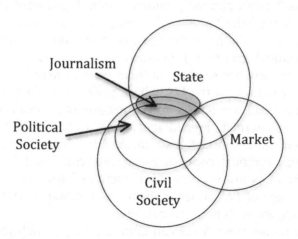

Figure 2.2 Journalists in Nineteenth-Century French Public Life

like the arts, the academy, and political groups (especially political parties). Thus, journalists were pushed in one direction by political society, which demanded that they participate in the scrum to influence public opinion. From another they were pulled by the state, which required journalists to assist in its efforts to manage public opinion. From yet another corner, journalists were pulled by the arts, and a notion of journalism as a literary enterprise. Even today, French journalists retain high literary ambitions, and relatively lower journalistic aspirations. The market represented a weak countervailing force to these pressures. In this context, individual journalists went about their work, and some of them became very powerful. But there was no *journalism*. The configuration of public life simply did not allow for its development. This is how the most advanced news system in the world in 1789 fell by 1900 far behind that of the US and UK.

The Development of the American Field

Between roughly 1900 and 1930, the United States experienced a revolution in the news (Barnhurst and Nerone, 2001; Ryfe, 2006; Matheson, 2000; Schudson, 1998). Newspaper front pages became more organized. Editors offered fewer stories on the front page, and now used headlines to convey editorial judgment. As a profession, journalism gained a higher social status. Reporters became more visible, and their activities became more uniform. Everywhere, reporters began to gather the same sorts of information from the same sources. They turned this information into news using the same devices: lede paragraphs, nut graphs, and the like. Their stories contained fewer voices than in the past. Authorities (such as public officials and experts) became more prominent, and everyone else faded from the scene. Within news stories, sentences became shorter and punchier, big on facts and short on narrative. Journalists began to hew to the same values, most of all to the principle of independence—from sources of information, from editors, and from audiences.

By 1930, more or less, this revolution was complete. A reader today would feel comfortable reading a front page from the 1930s. The news is more visual today; the writing is less formal and more interpretive. But like then, today's reporters get the same sorts of information from the same sources, and package this information in the same story forms as in the 1930s. A front page in an American newspaper from the 1930s has more in common with a front page from the twenty-first century than it does with one from 1900.

We have discussed above the broad strokes of how this happened. But how did it *really* happen, on the ground, in the lives of actual reporters? How did journalists create a new occupational field?

There is no better way to answer this question than to put oneself on the inside. Imagine then, that you are a young reporter for *The New York Times*. It is 1900, and Adolph Ochs, a young ambitious publisher, had just bought the *Times* four years before. For decades, it has been an "independent newspaper." This means your editor does not run for public office, but it also means that the paper strongly leans toward one of the parties, in this case, toward the Republican Party. Reporters who work for the paper are expected to convey this association in the news. Compared to party papers, *Times* reporters cover more and different kinds of topics, but party politics dominates the news, as it does for most every daily newspaper. Though your paper has no formal relationship with the Republican Party, much of the news reported in the paper comes from information received from the party. One description of a nineteenth-century reporter's job at the *Times* is that he transforms information obtained from party officials into news consumed by party members. As a young reporter, this is your inheritance.

You are about to participate in the creation of a new occupational field. This process is too large and varied to describe in full—at least from your singular perspective. So let's take a piece of it, and let it stand in for the rest. I have in mind the development of reporter source relationships between public officials and journalists. Out of these relationships flow a slew of practices, values, and associated roles that are integral to the field of journalism.

So here you are in 1900, at the beginning of this process. The *Times* is slowly freeing itself from the Republican Party, meaning that it no longer hews so closely to the party line. As this unfolds, however, it raises a new, unintended problem: if not from the party, where are you to find a reliable flow of information? If you needed a story in the past, you had only to visit the local party office. Where are you to turn now for such information? This is a problem of access and it vexes all newspapers as they move away from the party press model. As a young reporter, you have no interest in building a field of journalism. But if you are to be successful, you must solve the problems in front of you. This problem of access may be the most important, and raises a crucial point: reporters built the field of journalism by solving particular problems and taking advantage of specific opportunities.

For example, to solve the problem of access, you discover the burgeoning administrative state. In the twentieth century, government is tasked with responding to many more social issues and problems than in the past. This is especially true of the federal government, which, except for the period around the Civil War, had been relatively small and inconsequential. Moving forward, government will be very active in public life—without the aid of robust political parties. This means that public officials are also more active, and more intent on pushing public opinion behind their goals. It also means that government bureaucracies (and the numbers of bureaucrats) grow. The core beats of modern journalism revolve around these agencies, and this is no accident. After all, no other organization in society is better situated to provide journalists with a steady stream of information. Better yet, the information government agencies provide is free for the asking! Best of all, officials find that they need you as much as you need them. Remember, if they are to be successful, they must get citizens to support their initiatives. Well, how else are officials to accomplish this, except through the pages of newspapers? Newspapers are so important to government that these agencies begin to hire individuals—"public information officers"—whose job is precisely to provide you with newsworthy information. A good part of becoming a modern reporter comes to involve relationships with these government sources.

Out of this relationship spills any number of practices and

values central to modern journalism. Think, for instance, of the many rules associated with interviewing. Are we on or off the record? May I quote you for attribution? Are we on "deep background"? Answers to these questions mostly stem from official reporter relationships. Or, consider the machinations journalists adopt to avoid seeming to be too close to any particular source. Reporters begin to cast themselves as a "fly on the wall" at public meetings, independent of the interests of any particular source. They develop a habit of always speaking to more than one source. They stick to facts, and try to tell stories straight, with little or no bias toward any particular viewpoint. In fact, newspapers develop entire editorial processes to stamp out such biases. Out of official reporter relationships grows an entire tissue of news culture.

As a new reporter, you learn these new skills by patrolling a beat, which involves another set of new practices, like cultivating sources and perusing public documents. Soon, you become so successful at gathering information from government that you face another problem: it is not possible to print all of it. Newspapers are commercial enterprises, and so the number of advertisements run on a given day determines the number of pages a newspaper will publish. The space for news—the news hole—is defined as the part of those pages not taken up by ads. To fill this news hole, you have to make choices. Thus emerges one of the most vital of journalistic skills, knowing how to judge the newsworthiness of information.

Choices about newsworthiness inevitably lead to complaints: Why did you publish this story rather than that? Why did you use this source rather than another one? After all, no one elected you to filter communication between officials and the public. The more you serve as a mediator of public information, the more your credibility is put at risk.

To manage this problem, you innovate several new practices. For instance, you attribute all significant facts to a source. Doing so makes it clear that someone you have interviewed is claiming X, not you personally. You also seek out the most authoritative source for information. Why talk to a lowly police officer on the beat when you can talk to the chief of police? Why talk to a member of city hall when you can talk to the mayor? Why talk to a congressman when you can talk to the president? The more authoritative the source, the more your reporting seems credible. Finally, you begin to align the views expressed in the news to the range of views expressed by your sources, in other words, to conventional wisdom among policymakers. Doing so insulates you from the charge of bias and allows you to curry favor with those same officials.

It is true that some of these practices and values were invented decades before. But they gain new meaning in this new context. You improvise some of them yourself; others you borrow from fellow reporters. You take your new attitudes and practices with you from job to job. The most successful ones are codified in teaching manuals used in journalism schools, and conveyed to new reporters as part of their socialization into the newsroom. Professional journalistic associations emerge and disseminate the new practices as well. As this happens, the practices come to permeate the field.

In the process, practices and values that began as necessities (that is, solutions to problems) become virtues. For example, values like independence and objectivity began as pragmatic solutions to particular problems. Soon, however, they become normative commandments of the profession: thou shalt be independent! In this way, you come to share a normative worldview with other journalists. You now think of yourself as a "trustee of the public." You even find yourself claiming that you represent the public, and that much of your work is justified because the "public has a right to know." This is a new, elevated language for thinking about yourself and your activities, and you quickly embrace it.

This isn't to say, by the way, that all journalists embrace it equally, or at all. The field of journalism does not inflate in a uniform way. To see how and why this is so, it helps to return to the internal mechanics of social fields, to the process of justification and recognition we encountered in Chapter One. Imagine for a moment that it is now 1910, and another new reporter, fresh from a stint at one of the larger dailies, comes to the newsroom to teach you how to write a lede paragraph in the "who, what, when, where" style. Your natural reaction might be to ask: why should I write that way? His answer to this question must seem reasonable to you and to others: to your editors, to your publisher, to your sources, to the advertisers who will place their brands next to your copy, and to the audiences who will read your stories.

As I showed in the last chapter, these justifications eventually come to ground in the logics of contiguous social fields. For instance, when you ask, "Why should I write the paragraph this way?" he might respond: "Because it helps you write quickly." "Why is writing quickly so important?" you ask. "Because in this newsroom you are required to write on deadline," your fellow reporter retorts. "And why do I have to write on deadline?" you ask. "Because we have to fill the newspaper *every day* with stories!" he says. "Why don't we just put out a newspaper every other day, or only when there is news?" you naively ask. "Because this newspaper has contracts with advertisers that require it to run those ads every day!" he responds. Here, we see that the practice of writing lead paragraphs finds one ultimate justification in the logic of the market.

We now come to another crucial point: any particular practice may be justified in many ways, and the same justification may be used for many different practices. To capture this idea, Lamont and Thévenot refer to justifications for social practices as "repertoires of evaluation." They mean by this that any particular social actor—say a journalist—has at her disposal a repertoire of justifications for her actions. Social actors (journalists) turn to these justifications on the fly, in the midst of interaction, in an effort to convince others that what they have done is reasonable and legitimate.

For instance, a reporter might justify the "who, what, when, where" style through appeal to the logic of the state. She may say that readers rarely get past the first few paragraphs in a news story, and so, to ensure that they are well informed, reporters must include the most important information in the first paragraph. Or, she might appeal to the logic of the market: inverted-pyramid-style paragraphs are short, she argues, therefore efficient, and uniform and so transferrable across many different stories. She also has a professional logic at her disposal. Journalists, after all, are responsible for deciding what matters most in the events they cover, and to convey this material in a condensed, logical fashion. The range of justifications available to journalists depends on the constitution of the field. Journalists deploy these justifications in the stream of interaction, as they are called to account for their behavior. As they become more experienced, they develop a "feel for the game." That is, they learn which justifications are likely to work in what circumstances., and they learn where the boundaries of behavior lie: at the point where their justifications no longer seem reasonable to others. The field of journalism holds together not because journalists agree, but because they share an understanding of how to disagree, and which disagreements matter.

What have we learned from this exercise? Start with the fact that journalists everywhere face the same problems (of access, legitimacy, and sustainability), which guarantees that they will share a loosely held common sense. The fact that many work in similarly situated commercial news organizations lends still more regularity to the field. As the field of journalism becomes more ordered, journalists begin to recognize themselves in one another, and to compete with one another for status and influence. In this competition, a culture of journalism grows and deepens. The process of justification and recognition guarantees a degree of contingency in this culture. Journalists may justify any particular action in a number of ways, and their success of their actions depends on an ability to pull off the performance of justification with others.

The necessity of justification links journalism to contiguous social fields. The field of American journalism develops primarily across the market and the state, and less so across civil and political society (Figure 2.3). This location informs the 'repertoire of evaluation' that is at the disposal of journalists. For instance, commercial justifications are so common in American journalism because of its close proximity to the market. Similarly, it is no accident that journalism's cardinal value—objectivity—is often expressed in the vernacular of a progressive administrative discourse (Gans, 1978; Schudson, 1998), or that journalists come to imagine their practice, much as government bureaucrats do, as a kind of quasi-scientific expertise (Kovach and Rosenstiel, 2001). It is in this space that journalists develop a distinctive set of justifications. Some of these justifications become so deeply institutionalized that eventually they no longer require justification at all. They represent, in other words, constitutive assumptions of the field. In journalism, these are practices such as sourcing and attribution, and values such as objectivity, and roles such as being a "watchdog" of public officials. One cannot *be* a journalist without in some fashion adhering to these elements. Such institutionalization happens partly through path dependence: over time so many resources may accrue around a practice that the costs of change become prohibitive. It also happens when elements become implicated in the most charged of relationships: that between journalism and the state. It is no accident that journalists win most awards for activities associated with the state (for instance, for stories that lead to new laws or changed policies), and that the bestselling news story rarely gains much recognition within the field.

In 1900, you started as a cub reporter with more questions than answers about how to do journalism. In 1930, now a professional reporter, you sit back and reflect on what your generation has accomplished. Without intending to do so, you have invented a new occupational field!

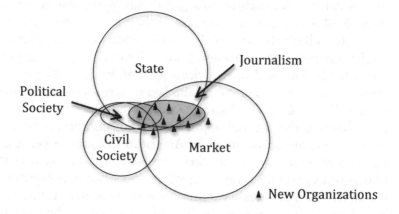

Figure 2.3 A Distribution of News Organizations across "Modern Journalism"

The Field of French Journalism

As Jean Chalaby (1996) argues, the field of journalism was a peculiarly Anglo-American invention. In noting as much, we should not exaggerate the similarities between American and British journalism. British journalists never embraced the ideal of professionalization, or a definition of objectivity as political neutrality, as strongly as their American counterparts (Hampton, 2004). Still, it is a historical fact that a mass market for news opened first in these countries. They were the most democratic societies in the world, meaning that they placed the fewest governmental strictures on the press., and it is in these countries that professionalization in journalism first took root. For these reasons, it is fair to say that the invention of journalism was an Anglo-American process.

The field of journalism took longer to develop elsewhere. In France, American news practices were well known by the early 1900s. But the constitution of the field in France made these practices impractical for most news organizations, and unpalatable to most journalists. Most obviously, the market for news in France remained very small. Policies enacted after World War Two were designed for this (Kuhn, 1995, Chaps. 1, 2). For instance, legislation was passed that set limits on the advertising rates newspapers could charge, and government adopted rules that limited the ability of news companies to become large and concentrated. The state also nationalized the nation's printing and distribution systems, and, perhaps more notably, nationalized the broadcasting system as well. Until the 1980s, it was not possible to practice television journalism independent of the state. The Fourth Republic also established a subsidy system for the press—one of the largest in Europe. This was done to ensure that many different political viewpoints could be expressed through the news. In the United States, new news practices were invented precisely to satisfy a growing market for news. News organizations in France had limited opportunity to participate in such a market, and so had little appetite for the new American practices.

French news organizations also had many opportunities in the political and civic fields. French politics remained much more ideologically diverse than in the US, meaning that many more and different kinds of groups vied for political power. These groups maintained a close connection to newspapers. For example, Chalaby (1996) reports that of the forty-six newspapers published in Paris after the war, forty "had a marked political tendency and *explicitly* defended a political doctrine" (p. 319, italics in original). Through the 1940s and 1950s, most political groups owned and operated at least one newspaper, and most newspapers hewed to a political doctrine. Operating in the civic and political fields meant that these groups had less interest in commodity news, and more interest in persuasive news: news that brought the organization's members together, or that attracted new adherents to the cause.

Part of French journalists' reaction to the American style surely stemmed from its inaccessibility. Even if they had wanted to, French journalists had little opportunity to practice journalism in the American manner. Most, however, had no such desire (Marzolf, 1984). Instead, they continued a long tradition of elevating the literary style. To most French journalists, grubbing for facts as American journalists did was unseemly and inane. For one thing, it missed the point of news, which was to enlighten and move to action. For another, it required little skill. Anyone could collect a fact from a press conference; few could write prose that moved people to action. Unlike American reporters, French journalists had little interest in acquiring a professional status.

This said, they did have an interest in becoming recognized as an occupation. By the 1920s, French journalists had their own trade union, and in 1935 the government passed a law recognizing journalism as a profession. Granted that the accreditation process was very loose—all that journalists had to show to be accredited was that they had written an article for any news organization— from then on they still had to be accredited by the Commission de la Carte d'Identité des Journalistes. Journalists also established Societies of Journalism, and the number of journalism schools increased as well. The field of French journalism grew, in other words; it just did so in fits and starts. From the beginning, it was more permeable than the American field, more open to the influ-

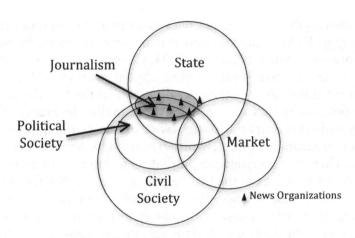

Figure 2.4   The Field of French Journalism

ence of the state and less secure in its autonomy. Even at its most developed, it came to have a different shape than in the US. Figure 2.4 visualizes the result (see also Benson, 2005, 2013). The state has always intervened more forcefully in the field of French journalism; exposed less to the market, the field is smaller. However, integrated more into civil and political society, it is more ideologically diverse.

Imagine for a moment that you are reporter in this field. What are the opportunities and constraints before you? Since many news organizations are associated more or less with a political group, most of your opportunities will come from this part of the field. These organizations are as interested in your ability to express and defend a political viewpoint as in your ability to gather and report facts. Another way to put this is to say that they are less interested in news as a commodity and more interested in its contribution to public debate. Like your American counterparts, you face the problem of access., and like them, you solve this problem by maintaining deep relationships with government sources. Unlike in the US, however, French authorities have more tools at their disposal for managing the news. They have more rules in place, and a long tradition of censorship when the rules fail. Your relationship with government is therefore fraught with more peril. In response, you are likely to be less confrontational than your American friends, and more cooperative (Chalaby, 2004; Charon, 1991). As in the US, you may achieve status in your chosen profession, but the criteria for doing so are markedly different. In the US, the most prized position is that of investigative journalist. In France, the literary journalist bears this status. None of this should imply that French journalism is absolutely different from its American counterpart. There are investigative journalists in France just as there are literary journalists in the US. Rather, it is to say that the fields share a family resemblance: they are similar, but not identical. The "repertoire of evaluation" available to French journalists is different from the American field because the problems and opportunities that lay before them are different.

The Form of News

Such differences are ultimately expressed in news—specifically, in the forms of news that are typical or conventional within a given field. In saying this, we should avoid absolute terms such as "always" or "never." Again, French and American news are different in important respects, but they are not absolutely different. There are advocacy journalists in the US who take their political role seriously, just as there are market-oriented journalists in France who write conventional commodity news. This said, many scholars have compared French and American journalism, and they have found significant differences (Alexander, 1981; Benson, 2002, 2013; Benson and Hallin, 2007; Esser and Umbricht, 2014; Hallin and Mancini, 2004). The primary differences are these: American news tends to be more fact-oriented and more neutral in tone. In comparison, French journalism is more likely to mix news and opinion, and to be more partisan. Among American journalists, there is also the belief that French journalism is less balanced than American journalism. However, Benson's (2013) content analysis of French and American immigration news suggests that this is not the case.

American journalists separate fact and opinion by making a distinction between news stories and op-ed pieces. Within news stories, they highlight facts through a practice of quoting and attribution: every significant fact is attributed to a source, which can be a document, but is often an individual to whom facts are associated via quotes. In the service of a broader narrative, journalists strongly mediate speakers' words, and introduce balance into their stories by including sources with different points of view, and ensuring that every story includes quotes that express these views. French journalism adopts what Benson (2013) refers to as a "debate ensemble" format. In part, this means that the major conflict within French journalism is often cast less as speaker vs. speaker and more as perspective vs. perspective. Compared to American journalism, French journalism contains more views across a broader array of organizations. French journalists allow speakers to express themselves more fully. Their stories are less fact-centered and more (for lack of a better term) point-of-view-centered. They are less formal and neutral in tone, and more apt to characterize perspectives.

Content analyses of news coverage indicate that these differences are systematic across American and French news. For instance, Esser and Umbricht (2014) find that American newspapers contained a "hard fact" structure 87 percent of the time in the 1960s, and 78 percent of the time in the 2000s. In contrast, French newspapers use the "hard facts" structure only 70 percent of the time over this same period (p. 237). Benson (2002) has a similar observation. In an analysis of national news outlets, he concludes, the "mixing of factual and normative writing" combined with less use of interviewing as an information-gathering technique continues to distinguish French journalism from its American counterpart (p. 63). Benson and Hallin (2007) agree. They show that French news stories are neutral in tone, on average, 70 percent of the time, while American news stories are neutral 95 percent of the time. These are differences in quality, not of kind. French newspapers use the "hard facts" structure a majority (70 percent) of the time, and about the same percentage of French news is neutral in tone. Such differences are not absolute. But they exist, and they persist over time.

71

One way these differences are expressed is in the institutional role each field takes up with respect to government. In the United States, journalists take on a watchdog role. This is expressed in the penchant of American journalists for investigative journalism. Even today, for American journalists, Woodward and Bernstein's investigation of the Watergate affair represents the epitome of journalistic excellence (Schudson, 1993). In contrast, French journalists are more politically engaged than their American counterparts. They are more likely, for this reason, to be critics rather than watchdogs. Benson and Hallin (2007), for instance, find that French news stories include more criticism of government than American news stories. This is largely due to the fact that French journalists are more likely to represent partisan, or at least politically engaged, news organizations. Yet French journalists have much less interest in investigative journalism (Charon, 1991; Rieffel, 1984). Chalaby (2004) notes that investigative journalism did not exist at all in France until the 1950s, and only became more common in the 1980s. Even today, however, "investigations remain practiced by an exceedingly small number of reporters," Chalaby writes, "as few media organizations have the resources to pay for lengthy research" (p. 1200).

After nearly two decades of research comparing French and American journalism, especially coverage of immigration news, Benson (2013) concludes this:

> In the United States, personalized "dramatic narrative" has become a dominant journalistic form, producing a tendency toward ... investigative reports and human interest profiles. In contrast, in France, a "debate ensemble" format is oriented primarily toward facilitating reasoned if often polemical debate and presenting multiple, diverse viewpoints. (p. 16)

The narrative style preferred by American journalists arises from their position in the market, where they must produce commodity news, and from a political system oriented around personality politics. French journalism's "debate ensemble" stems from its location in political and civil society, and from the state's strong intervention in the journalistic field.

Ultimately, these differences derive from slightly different notions of what journalism, and public life, are for. In the United States, journalists imagine that they inform citizens who are otherwise ignorant; in France, journalists imagine that they engage citizens who are already informed. When asked why they produce fact-oriented, balanced stories about public officials, American journalists argue that readers and viewers need to be given both sides of issues. Why do readers and viewers need both sides? They need both sides, journalists respond, so that they may form an opinion about the issues. Why do readers and views need to form opinions? So, journalists say, that those opinions may guide the actions of officials. Here, we come to a constitutive understanding of public life: officials act; citizens consume information and form opinions. In France, citizens are already pre-mobilized by an array of parties and political groups. As such, they are already informed, and already possess opinions. In this context, the point of journalism is not to inform, but to engage—specifically, to engage readers and viewers who know a great deal about the issues, and wish to discuss them, and see them discussed, in the news. Where Americans assume that public life is (or should be) dominated by expertise, the French understand public life to be defined by political contestation. These images of public life produce different "repertoires of evaluation" available to journalists as they justify their activities.

Conclusion

A comparison of French and American news has provided us an excellent opportunity to use the tools we developed in the last chapter. The location of journalism in public life opens particular sorts of problems and opportunities to journalists. As they act on these problems and opportunities, journalists begin to build a shared culture. The necessity of justifying one's actions—accounting to others for why one should do this rather than that—animates this process. Over time, journalistic culture gains integrity, which is another way of saying that journalists turn to, and accept, the same sorts of justifications for the same kinds of actions. As this happens, the boundaries of the field become sharper and its internal structure more organized. In the West, this process has produced a range of journalistic fields, all of which are different. The field of German journalism is different from the Danish field, is different from the Italian field, and so on. But they all share a family resemblance. Partly, this is due to the fact that elements of the Anglo-American field have migrated across Europe, and partly it is due to the fact that states in Western Europe are generally democratic, and economies are mostly market-based. Journalism, therefore, comes to have a similar look and feel.

Is the same true in other parts of the world? Does journalism share a family resemblance with the West in, say, China? Can the tools we have developed be used to answer this sort of question? It is to these questions that we turn in Chapter 3.

3

Outside the West

In recent years, scholars have begun to criticize the practice of applying Western concepts to non-Western societies (Curran and Park, 2000; Downing, 1996; Lee, 2015). The point is fair enough. Why apply a concept such as the public sphere to societies in which the term never developed? We shouldn't take this to mean, however, that comparisons between the West and non-West are impossible. Journalism, for instance, has developed in much of the world, and most everywhere it shares a family resemblance (Hallin and Mancini, 2012). This could not have happened without some common ground. From what we have learned in the past two chapters, that ground lies in public life. Journalism, after all, always emerges in the context of a public. In saying as much we should tread carefully. The public will have different histories and mean different things across societies. We must allow for these differences. Nonetheless, publics exist in many places, and where they exist journalism sometimes develops. Because this is so, the framework we have developed ought to be helpful in making sense of journalism outside as well as inside the West.

In this chapter, we will demonstrate as much in the context of a discussion of Chinese journalism. I have chosen China for several reasons. First, Chinese journalism demonstrates especially well Waisbord's (2013) point that the field of journalism is not fixed, but waxes and wanes. In 1920s republican China, journalism enjoyed a brief period of relative autonomy. This freedom dissipated entirely during the Communist period, only to be revived in the recent past. It also fluctuates across space. Journalism in China has grown in the last thirty years, but not uniformly. News organizations are more autonomous in some spaces of the field (especially in southern coastal cities) and restrained in others. Some journalists enjoy an autonomy similar to that felt by journalists in the West. Others are more constrained. Second, Chinese journalism deviates from the Western example in instructive ways. In many Western societies, journalism flourished first, and most consistently, in civil and political society. The same has not been true of China, where journalism mostly has emerged in the nexus between the state and the market. This difference is crucial for understanding the meaning of the practice in China. Finally, China is an interesting case study because the market has not had precisely the same sorts of effects on journalism in China as it has had in the West. In the latter—especially in the UK and US—the market often served as a counterpoint to the state, and so guaranteed the freedom of the press. Again, the same has not been true in China. Instead, market-driven journalism has been state-sponsored and regulated. The tools we have developed will help us understand the implications of this curious fact.

History

If a Western observer were asked to choose one word to describe Chinese journalism, it would likely be "censorship." Since the rise of the Communist Party of China (CCP) in 1949, journalism has first and foremost been the mouthpiece of the CCP. In fact, until the 1980s, only official news organizations were allowed to exist, and journalists could only distribute officially sanctioned party information. Journalists have also been the eyes and ears of the party. They keep watch over local bureaucrats, going so far, on some occasions, as to investigate abuses by lower-level party bureaucrats. In the form of restricted publications, available only to party leaders, they provide intelligence on local and regional happenings, and they generally monitor the public mood. They are also obligated to conduct "mass work," that is, to perform a kind of social work for Chinese citizens. Every newspaper, for example, maintains an office that citizens may visit to lodge complaints about abuses or misuses of government power. Journalists are assigned to investigate the matter, alert the appropriate state agency, and help citizens seek redress.

These roles have been formalized in state policy, and to ensure that journalists play them the state employs a legion of bureaucrats—which is putting it mildly. According to Nathan (1985, p. 69), by the time Mao died in 1976, the Chinese state included twenty-eight million bureaucrats, more than twenty million cooperative-factory officials, more than four million soldiers, and thirty-five million CCP members who drew their salary from the state. Any journalist found to violate the rules is subject to severe punishment (imprisonment and, in extreme cases, death).

Less well known is that this kind of formal censorship is relatively new in China. As Britton (1933) notes, China has had official news writing (in the form of "gazettes") since at least the T'ang Dynasty (618–906). Yet until the twentieth century China did not tax the press, had no licensing rules, and made no requirement that producers of news register with authorities. In fact, the first press censorship laws were not written until the early 1900s, and it was only in the latter stages of the republican period (roughly from the 1930s forward) that these laws were strongly enforced. This isn't to say that in earlier times news producers were free to write whatever they wished. In many ways, information was as tightly controlled then as it was during the Communist period. It is just that no formal laws were required to achieve this result. Understanding why this is the case lends insight into the structure of Chinese public life.

For two millennia before the twentieth century, China was ruled by a bureaucratic, patriarchal monarchy suffused with Confucian principles. Three of these qualities are easily explained. China was monarchical in the sense that a single imperial ruler held dominion. It was patriarchal because men led the state (and every other significant social organization), and these men treated those subject to their will as something akin to children. Finally, it was bureaucratic because Imperial rulers fashioned an elaborate bureaucracy, populated mostly by literate Confucian scholars and based upon a rigorous examination system, to regulate the broader society. It was this bureaucracy that constituted the "public" before which the ruler acted (Zhang, 2007). For instance, bureaucrats were the primary audience for Imperial news (in the form of gazettes). Further, bureaucrats were given the responsibility of educating the wider Chinese citizenry—essentially to socialize others into the practice of citizenship. Finally, Chinese bureaucrats—whose members congregated in the Imperial Court but also stretched across society—were granted the power of remonstrance, the power to complain to the monarch on behalf of ordinary Chinese citizens (Nathan, 1985).

The role of Confucianism in China is a bit more complicated. Confucianism has been called a religion and a philosophy, and it is probably a little of both. By the time of the Han Dynasty (206 BC–220 AD), it had become a primary set of organizing principles for Chinese society, and except for brief periods remained dominant through the nineteenth century. Without going into too much detail, the most basic Confucian principle is that human nature is inherently good, and that all people wish to find and express this goodness. A second principle is that expressions of this goodness are social, rooted in relationships between people, and especially in the public roles that people inhabit (such as father and mother, or farmer and politician)., and a third is that, through study and practice, individuals might learn to express this goodness in their lives, meaning that they may learn to play well the social roles they have been assigned. Proper guidance is key to this endeavor. As Nosco (2002) notes, Confucianism imagines individuals as enmeshed in a series of relationships, in some of which they act as benefactors (say, as fathers) and in some of which they act as beneficiaries (say, as members of a village). Beneficiaries are required to learn and obey, while benefactors are responsible for setting an example (living a good life), providing adequate instruction (moral suasion), and for structuring contexts so that the individuals in their care have an opportunity to discover and express their basic goodness. Beneficiaries and benefactors are obligated to one another. If beneficiaries fail to learn well, they may return to the proper path through instruction and criticism., and if benefactors—say, rulers—fail to live up to these responsibilities, beneficiaries have a right of remonstrance, or the right to complain and seek redress.

Because Confucianism imagines every social relationship as an intimate one, it has no conception of privacy. That is, it contains no sense of a private space outside of social obligations. In China, the opposite of "public" is not "private"; rather, it is "secret," a term that implies selfishness. Chinese thought also imagines few boundaries between formal associations, such as the state, and more informal ones such as voluntary associations or even families. Every corporate body, from the state to the bureaucracy to the landed gentry to the family clan, is imagined as one layer within a series of layers underneath the state (see Figure 3.1). Where Western societies imagine different arenas of public life in relation to (and sometimes in competition with) one another, Chinese society views them as nested, and as existing in a more or less harmonious relationship with one another.

Fei Xiatong's (1992) use of the metaphors "haystacks" and "ripples flowing from a splash in the water" illustrates in another way the difference between Western and Chinese societies. A Western-trained sociologist, Xiatong's analysis is a hallmark study of Chinese society. He argues that in the West society is often imagined as a collection of organized and individualized "straws"

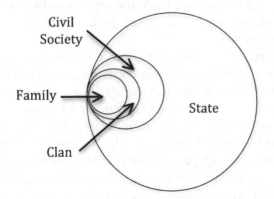

Figure 3.1 Public Life in Chinese Thought*
*Based on a similar illustration in Nosco, 2002: p. 338.

that form discrete groups, with clear boundaries and formal relationships. In contrast, the Chinese tend to view their society in terms of overlapping interpersonal networks that flow across organizations. Interpersonal ties precede organization, and so, in Chinese society, there are no formal boundaries between social layers. As the editors of Xiatong's book explain, "this is a society in which considerations of order, not laws, predominate; and in this context, order means . . . that each person must uphold the moral obligations of his or her network ties" (p. 24).

Through the nineteenth century, the Imperial ruler was seen as the ultimate benefactor within this social structure, someone responsible for leading an exemplary life, and for facilitating a path to goodness for his subjects. Citizens were responsible for becoming their best selves (that is, playing the role of citizen well), which meant in part obeying the ruler. Confucian thought sees no contradiction between these two directives (becoming one's best self and obeying the ruler), as obeisance and self-development are seen to act in harmony with each other. To be a good self in Chinese thought is precisely to do one's duty. This means that the entire range of social interactions is defined not by formal laws, but by ethical guidelines. If rulers and subjects act in appropriate ways, then there is no need for laws to be written down. Instead, people may lead and follow by example. Individuals who stray from the proper path are led back through example in the first instance, and shame (in the form of public criticism and self-criticism) in the second.

This social structure—that existed more or less unchanged for nearly 2,000 years—had profound consequences for the advent of journalism in China. Western missionaries are commonly credited with bringing journalism to Asia. Robert Morrison, a British missionary, was the first to arrive (in 1807), but by the 1830s missionaries had spread throughout China's coastal cities. They brought with them newspapers. Judge (1996) reports that between 1815 and 1894, roughly 150 foreign-managed, foreign-language newspapers, and an additional 70 foreign-managed Chinese-language newspapers were established (p. 19). Most of these newspapers appeared in coastal cities like Shanghai, and appealed in the first instance to the many foreigners who were gathering in these cities, and in the second to a growing middle class of Chinese officials and merchants. By the 1870s, a few Chinese merchants began operating their own newspapers (Judge, 1996), and thus modern Chinese journalism was born.

For a time, it seemed that Chinese journalism might simply adopt the Western model. Westerners trained many if not most early Chinese journalists (Lin, 1814/1968). Westerners also set up the first journalism schools in China (Volz and Lee, 2009; Weston, 2010), initially at Peking University in 1918, and in twenty-five other institutions by the mid-1930s. It is not surprising that many Chinese journalists trained in these schools began to act like their Western counterparts. For instance, they championed the principle of freedom of the press (and of speech). They also campaigned for public involvement in national affairs, and increasingly they purported to speak on behalf of the public (Gentz, 2007; Judge, 1996). By the late nineteenth century and early twentieth, they were principal actors in the reform movement within the Qing dynasty (1890s), in the revolution that followed (1911), and in the politics of the republican period (1912–49). For all intents and purposes, it appeared as if China was fast becoming a modern society in the Western mold, and Chinese journalism a modern institution along with it.

The Chinese people never gave up their longstanding sense of the organization of public life. In particular, even during the republican period Chinese thinkers held to the notion that society was, and ought to be, harmonious (Nathan, 1985). In their eyes, the rights of individuals added up to the rights of the whole; each person, when acting responsibly and legitimately, would naturally exercise his rights in ways that contributed to the greater good. When individuals acted selfishly, it was because they had not been socialized adequately to see, and act upon, the goodness inside them. It was the state's responsibility, and the responsibility of the bureaucratic class acting on behalf of the state, to socialize citizens in this way.

The Chinese viewed journalism through this lens (Judge, 1996; Mittler, 2004). Principally, this meant that they did not understand journalism to be a fourth estate residing outside of government. Rather, they imagined journalism to be an emissary of the state to the rest of society. The two roles can appear similar. In both cases, journalists were responsible for criticizing government and exposing official corruption. But Western journalists imagined themselves doing this on behalf of a public that stood outside of the state, that needed protection from the state. In contrast, Chinese journalists saw themselves performing an important state function, namely, helping the ruler set the best example possible for his citizens. As to their relationship with the broader public, journalists tended to view themselves as educators rather than defenders. The Chinese perceived no danger in having journalists play this role. To them, a well-organized society was one in which the state expressed the aggregate goodness of citizens. As the Chinese saw it, the role of journalists was to serve as a "hero-official," someone who helped the state and its citizenry achieve greater harmony (de Burgh, 2003b, p. 177). In this guise, journalists were charged in the first instance with obeying the ruler, and in the second with educating and socializing the Chinese people into their responsibilities as citizens.

Now we can see why China had no formal censorship laws before the twentieth century. If journalists strayed too far from their proper role, it was viewed as a personal (and not institutional) failure. The appropriate remedy, therefore, was to guide those who made mistakes back through the usual practices: instruction, example, public criticism, and the inculcation of shame. There was no need for formal censorship laws.

It was only in the twentieth century that the Chinese state began to adopt and implement formal propaganda campaigns and censorship laws. Ironically, it took the idea from the West. It is important to recognize that modernity did not so much emerge in China as land on its doorstep. When they opened the door, Chinese intellectuals were astounded and disturbed by what they found. How could China be so economically and technologically behind? And how could it catch up? In journalism the Chinese found one answer to these questions. From the very beginning, journalism in modern China was viewed as a state instrument for, as Nathan (1985) puts it, "seizing public attention." Primarily, this meant educating and socializing citizens to understand the need to modernize, and acting in ways that achieved this result. For this reason, "the voice of the press" in modern China has always been "properly polemical" (p. 149). The state turned to censorship law to ensure that journalism fulfilled this role. The first such law was written in 1906 and more were put on the books during the republican period. Not surprisingly, many journalists were arrested and periodicals closed. A few journalists were even assassinated. As MacKinnon (1997) observes, even in republican China—the most democratic moment in Chinese history—the press "always operated within the political system" (p. 18), and the political system operated in the context of the state.

When it took power in 1949, the CCP added a Marxist-Leninist gloss to this tradition. Journalism in this guise became the party's "vanguard," responsible for disseminating party doctrine and maintaining ideological conformity. But the impulse for journalism to play something like this role long predates the rise of the CCP. Journalism in China emerged and developed in the context of state institutions, in large part because for centuries the state has dominated Chinese public life. Other public institutions have developed in the shadow of this leviathan (for a discussion of Chinese civil society along similar lines, see Simon, 2013).

Markets

This history sets a context for what has transpired in Chinese journalism in recent decades. Beginning in 1979, and accelerating in the 1990s, China developed one of the largest markets for news in the world. Party leaders did not launch down this path because they had become converts to capitalism. Rather, by this time, the socialist state was simply running out of money. Part of the response of state leaders was to cut subsidies to many state organizations (including journalism), effectively introducing market principles into the economy. Slowly, in fits and starts, the state allowed a news market to emerge. At first, this meant allowing news organizations to collect and retain advertising revenue. Eventually, it meant the end of state subsidies for most news organizations, and a corresponding pressure on news managers to make a profit. Finally, it ended with the development of a vibrant news market in China that has become linked to the global economy.

Though journalism has been opened to market forces, those forces are still processed through party and state organizations. For example, all journalists must obtain a state license to practice journalism. Moreover, it remains illegal to operate an independent news enterprise in China. As Zhao (2008, p. 80) notes, every news organization must be "registered under a recognized institutional publisher or sponsor, which includes party committees, government bureaucracies, mass organizations, and other institutions of official standing." Since the party-state is organized in a regional, nested structure—moving from counties to provinces to the central state—so are the news media (Liu, 1971). National dailies are affiliated with national party committees, regional dailies with provincial committees, and so on, down to district-level newspapers and district-level committees. At each level, the state maintains propaganda and censorship agencies to ensure conformity to party principles. One of the consequences of this structure is a highly dispersed control system, one in which a multitude of political actors and agencies have a hand in monitoring the media (Tsui, 2003; Zhao, 2008). Another is that the conglomeration of Chinese media has mostly been regional in scope (Lee, He, and Huang, 2006). Any effort to create truly multinational media companies would entail transferring resources from one regional group (and government) to another—a potentially huge economic and political loss (Hu, 2003).

Despite the continued role of the state in news production, marketization has had a number of predictable consequences. One is that the sheer amount of news produced has expanded (Chan and Qui, 2001). At the beginning of the reform period in 1979, China had sixty-nine newspapers. By 2005, that number had grown to more than 2,000 (Shirk, 2011, p. 10)., and what had once been an industry reliant on state subsidies had by 2005 amassed revenues exceeding $40 billion per year (Gang and Bandurski, 2011, p. 38). In the same period, television experienced a ninefold increase in the number of stations operating around the country (Di, 2011). Every other medium, from magazines to the Internet, experienced the same kind of growth (Lee, 1994).

Another is an increase in sensational news. Sensationalism involves a shift from hard news (policymaking, political, and economic news) toward soft news (such as entertainment and consumer news). Sensational stories focus on the personal troubles and foibles of individuals, and tend to be overly dramatic and moralistic. When directed at politics, sensational news tends to focus on political scandal—on the malfeasance of individual politicians. All of these features characterize the commercial media in China. Newsstands on the streets of Chinese cities are filled with tabloids that feature blaring stories of scandal—literally blaring as loudspeakers are attached to them. The scandals often involve celebrities, and are told in melodramatic, purple prose (Lee, 2000; McCormick and Liu, 2009; Zhao, 2000). In a similar way, soap operas, crime shows, and reality shows compose an increasing share of commercial television in China (Zha, 1996).

But a third seemingly natural consequence has not occurred. News markets have not loosened the state's control of journalism to any great extent. Let me qualify that statement: *some* relaxation of state control has occurred. Journalists as a whole probably enjoy more autonomy today than at any time since the 1920s and 1930s. This is especially the case for journalists working on subjects somewhat removed from politics (such as food and culture, entertainment, and economics). Such journalists operate in the market with little official interference. Still, the state closely monitors political news, and even journalists who write on topics seemingly removed from that subject can find themselves in trouble with official censors. These censors work at every level of media and government. They exercise control mostly by issuing guides as to what should or could be published on a given topic. In the case of particularly sensitive issues, however, censorship may be more overt. After publishing information banned by the government, it is not uncommon for editors to be removed from their posts, or for journalists to lose their jobs. This issue of censorship is complicated by the fragmented nature of the system. Journalists may be banned by one level of government from publishing certain information only to be encouraged by another level of government to publish the same information. Still, the overall atmosphere of censorship in Chinese journalism is striking. Just as an illustration of the current situation, in its 2014 ranking of press freedom around the world the Freedom House rated China 184 out of 197 countries. Markets, it seems, have not set up journalism as a counterpoint to the state.

Today then, Chinese journalism can appear paradoxical. On the one hand, the Communist Party of China (CCP), which has ruled China since 1949, strongly censors the press. This is less true than before 1979, when restrictions began to loosen, but today it is still common for journalists to be arrested, or lose their jobs, for something they have written (e.g., Zhao, 2008). On the other hand, practices such as investigative journalism have never been stronger in China (Tong, 2007; Tong and Sparks, 2009; Hassid, 2008). Chinese journalists are exposing more instances of official corruption than ever before. Strangely enough, they are sometimes spurred to do so precisely by the state officials who otherwise censor their work. On still another hand, Chinese journalists embrace professionalism more than at any time since the 1920s (Zhang and Su, 2012). Yet "paid journalism"—the practice of sources paying journalists for stories—remains quite common even as journalists embrace professional values. In part because of paid journalism, and in part because they are so strongly censored by the state, Chinese journalists are not trusted by the public. That said, journalists are part of an esteemed class of intellectual-writers whose history stretches back over two millennia. Even today this history lends the profession a certain aura. Taken together, it appears that Chinese journalists are mouthpieces of the state, tribunes of the people, intellectual-writers, worker bees, and esteemed professionals—all at the same time!

Scholars of Chinese journalism have strained to make sense of this complexity. Mostly, they have approached it in terms of a tension between journalism's historical role as a mouthpiece of the party, and the more recent rise of market-based news. The natural question posed by this binary is "how far?": how far will journalism stray from party control to become an independent, autonomous profession, insulated from state interference by the market, capable of truly informing the public, and of holding the state accountable for its policies (Chan, 2003; Chu, 1994; Hong, 1998; Lee, 1990, 1994; Polumbaum, 1990; Zhao, 2008)? As Xin (2012) points out, this question has as its backdrop the Western experience in which the advent of markets more and less had this consequence for journalism (see also Curran and Park, 2000; Downing, 1996). Yet, it is a narrative that does not seem to be playing out in China. If traditional approaches to journalism are inadequate for explaining the situation in China, perhaps new tools may help.

The Chinese Field of Journalism

As a start to developing these tools, Pan (2000; and Lu, 1994) has argued that Chinese journalism is structured by four discourses, which he labels "party-press," "Confucian intellectual," "professionalism," and "market economy." In his account, journalists and news organizations negotiate local circumstances by improvising in and around these discourses. For him, the question is not whether journalism is state-sponsored *or* market-based, but how actors manipulate discursive resources to solve local problems. We may extend and formalize Pan's approach using the concepts we developed in Chapter One. In our vernacular, the discourses Pan identifies consist of logics that stem from different arenas of public life: Confucianism from civil society and the state, the party-press from the state, professionalism from journalism, and the market economy from the market. The field of journalism has inflated in the midst of the pushing and pulling among these logics. In this environment, news production is a strategic, improvisational act shaped by the pushing and pulling felt by individuals and organizations in the field. The "game of Chinese journalism," then, is defined by rules and resources forged to play this particular game.

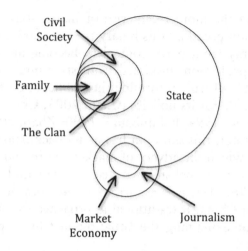

Figure 3.2 Market-Based Journalism in Chinese Society

Figure 3.2 visualizes this situation. It places the market both inside and outside of the state. It is inside the state because, in formal terms, the state owns the market. It is outside the state because once the market was allowed to emerge, its logic began to exercise force in Chinese society. This is the case even though the government formally owns Chinese journalism. As we know, journalism inflates in the friction between the market and the state. Before the advent of markets, Chinese journalism did not exist, mainly because no countervailing force to the state existed, and so no significant distinction was made between journalism and government. After 1979, news organizations began to be thrust into the market, and a new dynamic took hold. Even then, state officials might have wished to continue using reporters as stenographers. But editors and reporters now had a new reservoir of justifications for why they should be given more freedom. They could assert that the market demands it. Here is how one news executive put this point to Liu (2012): "Some people think that maybe our steps [in investigative reporting] are too big, that we are trying to get people's attention by saying something impressive. But frankly, we have to do this, otherwise there is no market" (p. 94). In a market, profits can be made only if customers are found and satisfied. Therefore, if news audiences wish for journalists to hold government more accountable, then that is the direction in which news organizations will be pushed. Since 1979, this logic has only become stronger.

Market logic has an influence even on news organizations directly connected to the state, like the Xinhua News Agency. Xinhua is the official news agency of the state and the *People's Daily* is the state's official newspaper. Yet as the state has pushed commercialization, Xinhua has found itself pressured to respond to audiences. As Xin (2012) reports, marketization has forced Xinhua to relinquish its role as a regulator of international news so that it can compete more directly with international news agencies. Marketization also has led Xinhua to restructure its operation so as to give local news outlets more control over financial and editorial decisions. These changes have allowed journalists like Zhou Yijun, a longtime reporter for Xinhua, more control over everyday news decisionmaking. Her "biggest reward," she has told one interviewer, "[is to do] stories that . . . lead to change. . . . Your reporting should move people and motivate people to change the world" (Polumbaum, 2008, p. 33).

The influence of markets on official news organizations suggests that logics of public life do not exercise force in a mechanistic way. It is not accurate to say that the market simply pulls news organizations in an opposite direction from the state. The situation is more complicated than that. Much of the complication is due to the role of interpersonal networks in Chinese society, and to the very different structural relationship between markets and the state in China. Specifically, state actors have directed the growth of markets in China. For example, they play a strong role in Chinese capital markets and most bank assets are still owned by the government (Chen and Dickson, 2010). Government agencies at every level also direct the allocation of financial resources in ways not practiced in Western industrialized democracies, and crediting agencies are strongly influenced by the government. To thrive in the Chinese economic environment, strong political ties are a must. Entrepreneurs often have backgrounds in state-run industries, and use their government connections to succeed. In

China, this is to say, the private economy remains nested to a great extent within the state. The same is true of journalism, and similar consequences follow. The intermingling of market and state forces within the interpersonal networks of journalists shape the reservoir of rules to which journalists might appeal to justify their actions.

Scholars have tended to flatten this intermingling by describing the situation in either/or terms: journalists are either watchdogs or party mouthpieces (Hassid, 2008; Yuezhi, 2010). Either the state intervenes or the market grants journalists a measure of autonomy. This frame is sometimes correct. The state can and does squelch journalistic autonomy on occasion. But in many cases this frame mischaracterizes the situation. Sometimes, it is the market that squelches professionalism in journalism; sometimes it is the state that supports it, and sometimes both work together against journalistic autonomy. The either/or frame makes it difficult for scholars to reflect the situation of Chinese journalism in all its complexity.

Consider the practice of paid or "red envelope" journalism (Dai, 2013). It is common for Chinese journalists and news organizations to accept money in exchange for favorable news coverage. This practice may take many forms (Li, 2013). It may involve payment from a government bureaucrat for travel or meal expenses. It may involve "advertising fees" placed directly into a news organization's bank account. It might even take the form of outright bribery: "If you do not pay me [state bureaucratic or business manager] I will write this story!" Generally, payments are designed either to ensure positive coverage or suppress negative coverage.

In the West, this practice is interpreted as simple corruption that can never be justified. If a journalist is caught taking money in return for news copy, she will immediately be fired. In China, the situation is not so clear. Many observers in China condemn the practice in just this way, as wholly unacceptable on all occasions (Epstein, 2008). Often, however, paid journalism may be justifiable. Put yourself in the position of a Chinese journalist. You have just attended a press conference at which a local business or government agency has publicized the launch of a new economic initiative (say a new policy or a new product line). You have taken a red envelope and plan to write a story praising the new initiative. A Western observer pulls you to the side and asks why you do this. After all, aren't you engaging in corruption and contradicting the values of your profession? How might you respond?

One response might be that your job is to promote the economy. It is state policy to foster private enterprise, and as an "emissary from the state," you should do everything you can do to push this policy forward. Here, your justification derives from journalism's traditional role as a "supervisor" of public opinion. Given that the official state policy is to promote the market, taking money to serve this cause may be justified. Alternatively, you might say that your story will educate citizens about how such product lines are developed. Given their Communist past, it is important for citizens to understand how the private economy works, and how innovation takes place. In this instance, your justification ends with a more Confucian conception of journalism's role, that of guiding or educating the public. Or, you might say that this is how you make a living. The state wishes workers to be more entre-preneurial, and paid journalism is certainly that. In fact, many journalists depend on it for their livelihood. As news organizations have transitioned to a commercial system, journalists increasingly have become contractors paid by the piece. To make ends meet, they often take second jobs or accept money in exchange for copy. You might even argue that the practice gains you important political and social connections, and it provides you access to better sources. Both of these outcomes make you a better reporter. It also, in a curious way, makes you more economically self-sufficient, especially from your editors. Taking these payments, you may argue, enhances your professional status!

Notice that these justifications end in constitutive rules, or state-ments about what journalists are, and are for. In the first instance, journalists are supervisors of public opinion. In the second, they are emissaries of the state. In the third, they are entrepreneurs, and in the fourth they are savvy reporters connected to key sources in their communities. These rules define what journalism is, and is for. In some ways they are similar to models of journalism that exist in other societies. For instance, American journalists sometimes imagine themselves as educating citizens, or as entrepreneurs. In this way, journalism everywhere shares a family resemblance. However, as with the Confucian overlay onto what it means for journalists to educate the public, in many ways they are distinctive to Chinese society—a society in which the state looms large over public life, even to the extent of shaping markets.

Notice also that the constitutive rules of Chinese journalism do not place the market or the state in a fixed position vis-à-vis journalism. By regulating paid journalism, the state may buttress the profession by insulating it from market forces, just as markets may detract from it when advertisers pay reporters. This is to say, more contingency exists in the way that the game of Chinese journalism is played than a simple "state vs. markets" frame can account for.

While we are rethinking the role of contingency in the journalistic field, we might also reconsider the nature of boundaries to action. It is surely the case that while contingency exists in the field, the rules and resources available to Chinese journalists are not entirely elastic. There are limits to the actions journalists may justify. What are these limits? Properly understood, the answer is that limits lie in a shared understanding of what counts as what in Chinese journalism. More simply, they lie in constitutive rules. Let me explain with an example. In September 2014 eight Chinese journalists working for a business news website, 21st Century Net, were arrested for taking payoffs from companies in exchange for flattering coverage. Apparently, the company took upwards of $50 million from more than 100 companies. Typically, the state has allowed business newspapers more autonomy than politically oriented newspapers. So why were these people arrested? Partly it has to do with the scale of the payments: $50 million is a lot of money! And partly it has to do with timing. At present, the state is focused on corruption as a hindrance to the economy. These arrests allow the state to demonstrate that it takes the issue seriously. Whatever the reason, these journalists met the limits of justification available within Chinese journalism. They were not able to convince others that, in this instance, taking cash for news coverage was legitimate and appropriate. Put another way, they found themselves standing outside the field of journalism, no longer members of a common understanding of what journalism is, and is for. It is not always possible to recognize where these boundaries lie, but it is easy to see when they have been crossed. The ultimate limit on action, then, is recognition: the ability to take a given action and persuade others that it is a recognizable instance of the practice.

Part of the difficulty in keeping a balance between contingency and determinism, it seems to me, is the spatial language that naturally lends itself to a discussion of social fields. Words such as "near" or "close," "boundaries" or "parameters," are often used to visually describe social fields. With respect to journalism, it seems intuitive to suppose that the closer a news organization is to the center of the state, or the economy, the more strongly it will be shaped by the logic of that field. Organizations and individuals positioned differently in the field will act in different ways. In many cases, this is true, but it is not always true. Spatial metaphors can be misleading when thinking about social fields. To demonstrate as much, and to offer an alternative way of thinking about fields that hinges on the concept of resources, let me end this chapter with a brief discussion of investigative journalism in China.

Investigative Journalism

No single definition of investigative journalism exists. Generally, however, it is news that attempts to document and remedy injustice, to hold powerful institutions and people accountable for their actions (Ettema and Glasser, 1998). Defined this way, we may assume that investigative journalism does not exist in China. After all, Chinese journalism remains even today the mouthpiece of the state. Its nearness seems to imply that journalism will not under any condition conduct investigations of the state. From the mid-1980s forward, however, investigative journalism in China has become quite common (Bandurski and Hala, 2010; Svensson et al., 2014; Tong, 2011). Journalists now routinely uncover abuses perpetrated by public officials, document environmental hazards,

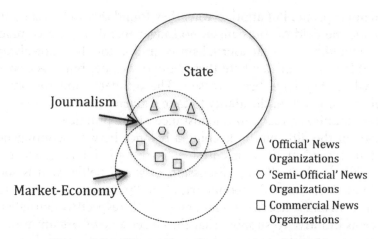

Figure 3.3 Chinese News Organizations in Public Life

and investigate the activities of private enterprises. Learning this, we might suppose that its rise is due solely to the growth of commercial news organizations. The idea here is that the market opens a space in which journalists can be more autonomous from the state. It turns out that this conclusion is too simplistic. In China, state-run news organizations often produce investigative journalism and commercial news organizations often avoid it. Explaining how and why this is the case helps us to see a very important point about social fields generally, and journalism specifically.

Let's begin with Figure 3.3. It presents a close-up view of the field of Chinese journalism. Here we see three types of news organizations (Stockmann, 2013, p. 67). "Official" news organizations are sponsored directly by a party or governmental institution and their leaders are almost always political officials or party members. Commercial news organizations have no state affiliation and are distinguished by the fact that their primary, often sole, source of income comes from advertising. Party or governmental institutions sponsor semi-official news organizations, and their leaders are often party or state officials, but these organizations are also required to take in advertising and make a profit. These three types span across media, but it is fair to say that TV stations generally are more official than not, and the vast majority of non-official news organizations are print-based (either newspapers or magazines).

When graphed this way, it appears that official news organizations are least likely to produce investigative journalism because they are nearest to the state. Here, *nearness* implies strength, specifically, the strength of force exercised on official news organizations by the administrative logic of the state. However, it is not nearness per se that matters, but the *amount of resources that pool around particular practices* in specific organizations. The question, then, is not one of closeness, but one of measuring the amount of various resources associated with investigative journalism that have pooled within particular news organizations.

This way of thinking opens us to recalling the unique history of Chinese journalism and its relationship to the state. As we learned above, historically, journalists in China have considered themselves Confucian intellectuals (de Burgh, 2003a, 2003b) who bear a responsibility to investigate social ills and educate the citizenry. This is a kind of symbolic resource—a tradition—that has pooled within journalism to support investigation of public abuses. It intersects with another symbolic resource, the liberal journalistic tradition of the early twentieth century (Tong, 2011, p. 20), which also imagines reporters as "supervisors of public opinion," responsible for holding officials accountable. As for the Communist period, it is important to remember that journalists not only are the mouthpiece of the CCP, they are also its eyes and ears. The latter role requires them to investigate public complaints and forward their findings to appropriate state agencies (Liebman, 2005). Coupled with the Confucian and liberal traditions, the eyes and ears tradition of journalism under the CCP means that material and symbolic practices associated with investigative journalism may be deeply embedded within official news organizations.

If you found yourself in one of these newsrooms, what would these resources look like? They would take the form of know-how: there will be journalists on staff who are highly skilled at conducting such investigations. They would take material form, as in staff lines: some of these newsrooms will maintain an investigative team; others will have resources sufficient to pay journalists to conduct months-long investigations. It would take the form of status: other journalists will hold investigative journalists in high esteem. It would take the form of values: editors will place a high value on conducting such investigations and encourage their staff to do this sort of reporting. In these and similar ways, investigative journalism will have taken root in newsrooms.

The upshot of our discussion is that these resources not only exist in official newsrooms; they may have been institutionalized over a long period of time. More than this, the state often has an interest in mobilizing these resources. Earlier, we learned that the state is not nearly as monolithic as one might assume (Svensson et al., 2014; Zhao, 2008). With the onset of reform, the national government has decentralized power to a great extent, meaning that many state agencies and many levels of government now possess a degree of autonomy and authority. This has made it more difficult for national party leaders to oversee the vast apparatus of government, especially at the local level. It also has introduced policy competition between bureaucrats, and, because political society is nested within the state, bureaucrats also compete with one another to shape public opinion. In this context, leaders have begun to strategically promote investigative journalism. National party leaders invite journalists to investigate the activities of local bureaucrats; state agencies direct their news outlets to investigate the actions of other state agencies (Lorentzen, 2013)., and official news organizations have the material resources to satisfy these demands (Huang, 2004). They do not receive nearly the subsidies they once did, but these organizations remain closely tied to party and state institutions, and so have at their disposal a range of resources not available to purely commercial organizations.

Beginning in the 1990s, the interests of state and party leaders began to catalyze the pool of resources available to official news organizations—and investigative journalism bloomed. First in programs such as *Focus,* which aired first on China Central Television (CCTV) in the mid-1990s, which was broadcast on CCTV and then on more than sixty other television stations through the 1990s (Tong, 2011, p. 39; Xiaoping, 2002), investigative journalism found a home in a seemingly unlikely place: official news outlets. Investigative journalism, this is to say, arose directly out of the administrative logic of the state.

Of course, it did not only flourish there. In print media, commercial weeklies and dailies such as *Southern Weekend* also began conducting investigations. These newspapers, which were concentrated in southern coastal cities (Shen and Zhang, 2013, 2014), enjoyed more relaxed oversight from local propaganda departments. They also found that investigations were key to establishing credibility with an audience. As Pang Zinzhi, mid-1990s editor-in-chief of the *Dahe Daily*, put it: "To practice public opinion monitoring was the most efficient way to occupy the market. It was a period in which we could accumulate capital" (Tong, 2011, p. 61). To this extent, the logic of the market pushed journalists in these newsrooms to adopt a critical, even antagonistic, posture toward the state (Lin, 2012).

The state may censor investigative journalism, but commercial newsrooms are not always sympathetic to the practice either. Western observers have worried about this fact in their own societies for decades (Greenwald et al., 2000). For one thing, commercial news organizations may come to the conclusion that investigative journalism is simply too expensive. It costs a great deal of money to pay a team of journalists to work on a single project for months at a time. When profit margins are slim, news managers may have less interest in supporting deep investigative work. The practice may also threaten a news organization's relationship with key advertisers. Few news companies can afford to get on the wrong side of the folks who pay their bills. It is also often the case that local businesses have strong ties to local state bureaucrats. Offending the one group may be tantamount to offending the other, and so may trigger unintended political consequences. In this instance, the state and market may work together against the practice (Stockmann, 2013; Zhao, 2000).

Several observers argue that 2003 represents the apex for investigative journalism in China (Chan, 2010; Tong, 2011). Since that time, the state has cracked down harder on the practice. It has issued more guidelines, appointed more censors, and generally harassed investigative journalists more than at any time since the

1970s. At the same time, commercial news organizations have shown less appetite for investigations. Their reluctance is partly due to a wish to avoid the wrath of government censors. It is also a consequence of a simple economic calculation that such investigations are bad for business. Together, market and state forces have created a more hostile environment for investigative journalism.

Even so, the practice remains "sticky" (Bandurski and Hala, 2010; Svensson et al., 2014; Tong, 2011; Tong and Sparks, 2009). Put another way, sufficient resources have pooled around the practice to lend it resilience. These resources have been embedded in journalism schools, for instance, where the practice is routinely taught (Xu et al., 2002). Journalists have gained the requisite skills, and journalists and editors appear dedicated to its persistence. They are also highly valued by journalists within the field, lending any journalist who exhibits them a measure of esteem. Moreover, the conditions that led party and state leaders to support the practice have not entirely dissipated. The same can be said for pressures on commercial news organizations to satisfy audience demand. Together, these conditions have kept the practice alive.

The fact of its persistence means that investigative journalism can still be justified in China. Such justifications, however, are contingent. They depend on a variety of factors that journalists must weigh when they choose to engage in the practice. As Tong (2011, pp. 143–4) describes, when journalists learn of an issue on which they might conduct an investigation, they must decide whether the story is suitable. This entails considerations such as: Can they gain access to the right information and the right sources? Do they have the time and resources to do the story justice? Once they decide to investigate the issue, they must convince their editors to go along. These editors must balance other considerations: Is the story timely, or more often, untimely? Does it pose too much political danger to the organization? Is it too expensive? Different departments—say, the political department and the commercial department—may weigh into the conversation with their own considerations. If party censors hear of an investigation before it is published, they may also get involved. The entire interaction is contingent, meaning that at any moment a news organization may self-censor, or a story may be censored by a party or state organization.

This contingency is ordered and organized by rules, and, as Pan (2000) notes, the journalists involved learn how to deploy these rules in particular situations. Some of the rules are informal. They exist as rules of thumb that "everyone knows." For instance, it is widely understood that journalists should report the truth. This is a powerful justification for investigative journalism: If asked to justify their actions, journalists may respond that they simply wished to uncover the truth. That said, there are many truths. Which ones journalists choose to uncover depends a great deal on circumstance. In part, it depends on other informal rules, like one that suggests that journalists should confine themselves to uncovering abuses (or truths) at the same level of government as their news organization. A district newspaper should not investigate regional officials, and a regional newspaper should not highlight the activities of national bureaucrats (Repnikova, 2014). Another "rule" is that local journalists rarely have sources in upper levels of government. When considering whether to conduct an investigation, journalists must determine whether the information will be available to complete the project. Some rules have a more formal cast. In 2005, the government issued a new rule prohibiting cross-regional investigations, that is, investigations by one regional news outlet about events occurring in another region. Local and regional officials encouraged this rule for, while they might censor reports in their own area of influence, they could not stop reports of their activities from being published in other regional news outlets. Using this loophole, reporters often investigated the abuses of their own officials, and then, to escape censure, fed the information to reporters working in other regions. Even this formal rule, however, is flexible. National leaders often want journalists to uncover local abuses of power, and it is difficult and costly to enforce. So, despite the rule, journalists will sometimes conduct cross-regional investigations.

Whether a given investigation is conducted, then, depends on many things. It depends on the level of resources available and on the ability of the people involved to read the context well enough that they mobilize the right justifications for the right people, and so persuade one another that the investigation is appropriate and legitimate. Journalists deploy such rules creatively, on the fly, in response to local circumstances. As justifications, however, the rules are not random. They have been institutionalized within the field over time, in response to the particular sorts of problems Chinese journalists face. Those problems are defined by the characteristic pushing and pulling among the market, the state, and the profession in China. Journalists demonstrate their competence (their membership in the community of reporters who occupy the field) by their ability to understand and wield these rules. The limits to action lie at the boundary of recognition—specifically, at the point when an action can no longer be justified as a legitimate instance of the practice.

It is true that some of these rules are similar to those deployed in other societies. All journalists justify their actions, for instance, by claiming that they are only seeking the truth. To this extent, journalism everywhere shares a family resemblance. But the rules and resources available to Chinese journalists are distinctive. They have emerged and built up within a configuration of public life that is unique to China. Chinese investigative journalism shares a family resemblance to the practice elsewhere, but it is not precisely the same.

Let me end this section by adding a final layer of contingency to this process. Many scholars argue that investigative journalism in China mostly confirms the administrative logic of the state (Zhao, 2004). For example, Stockmann (2013, p. 13) asserts that marketization has done little more than make "propaganda for sale." With the advent of market-based news, it is no longer necessary for the state to control all news outlets to achieve its overall goals. Instead, it may allow commercial news organizations a limited sphere of autonomy. These organizations may be freed to report on abuses by local officials, for instance, or to investigate issues on which the national government wishes to force change. This limited autonomy (as compared to official news outlets) enhances their credibility in the eyes of audiences, and so, according to Stockmann, only serves to reinforce party control more strongly.

"Propaganda for sale," he concludes, "strengthens the ability of media to communication societal feedback to authoritarian leaders and disseminate information . . . in a direction favorable to CCP rule" (p. 14).

Put in terms of our toolkit, Stockmann suggests that investigations motivated by the administrative logic of the state must necessarily end in reproducing that logic. This no doubt happens, but it is an empirical matter and not an ironclad law. One can easily imagine an internal investigation being leaked to the wrong news source or an investigative journalist going further than his government sponsors wished or an investigation of local officials metastasizing into a national scandal. In the transfer from administrative logic to investigation to publication, in other words, mistakes can be made. Just because an investigation is imbued with the administrative logic of the state does not mean its consequences *necessarily* reproduce that logic. This fact adds a last layer of contingency to the journalistic field. Not only is it impossible to predict entirely which investigations can be justified, once completed it is also impossible to predict their consequences. Each action is an intervention in the field produced by a particular juxtaposition of people, rules, and resources. It is an empirical question whether any one of these juxtapositions ends in reproducing state power.

Conclusion

In Chapter One, we learned that public life is organized into distinctive arenas. Each of these arenas contains a logic: a set of privileged norms, practices, identities, and so on. As a social field in its own right, journalism inflates in the pushing and pulling between these logics. One might argue that this image of journalism is more useful for understanding journalism as practiced in the West than elsewhere. After all, the approach follows directly from the Western experience. In this chapter, however, we have seen that Chinese journalism is also graspable in terms of its relationship to the public. In China, journalism is shaped by the overwhelming importance of the state in shaping public life. The sorts of rules (for example, a journalist should conduct investigations of officials who work at the same governmental level as the newspaper) and resources (that is, the notion of a journalist as a "supervisor of public opinion") available to Chinese journalists are strongly shaped by this configuration of public life.

Getting outside the West has an added benefit. Confined to the Western experience, it is tempting to view journalism's relationship to the public purely in spatial terms, but the Chinese case shows that this is dangerous. Perhaps because it is so different from the Western experience, China demonstrates the inherent fluidity of public life. In China, the boundaries of public life hinge on interpersonal ties that connect individuals to networks of relationships. Recognizing this fluidity alerts us to the danger of easy assumptions, such as the idea that because a news organization is market-oriented it necessarily will be dominated by the logic of the market. This assumption may be true, but it is also possible that rules and resources more directly tied to the state may exercise a strong gravitational pull even in market-oriented news organizations. Whether or not this is true in a particular instance is an empirical question, and cannot be predicted by theory alone. Instead, researchers must untangle the actions and justifications that flow from particular interactions. The same is true when thinking about journalism's boundaries. These boundaries are not fixed; they arise in moments of interaction. In particular, they lie at the limits of recognition. In the case of Chinese investigative journalism, they are raised at the moment when actions taken by journalists can no longer be justified as legitimate or appropriate instances of the practice.

Now that we are on a discussion of boundaries, and the limits of recognition, I want to turn to a consideration of normative theory. It is here, I think, that we find a deep pool of resources for delimiting the boundaries of the journalistic imagination. This is the topic of Chapter Four.

4

The Journalistic Imagination

In a stocktaking essay, Blumler and Cushion (2013) lament the increasing marginalization of normative theory within journalism studies. "If journalism studies becomes too insular," they write, "and becomes fixated on the practical world of news production ... then the fundamental relationship journalism has with civic values could become a rather distant concern" (p. 262). This argument hinges on a distinction between practice and values. Either researchers study "the practical world of news production," or focus their attention on the "relationship journalism has with civic values." While this frame is understandable, it presents a stark choice that may be unwarranted. In fact, it may be that practice implicates values (and vice versa)—so much so that it is impossible to understand the one without consideration of the other.

In this chapter, we will examine the relationship between normative accounts and journalistic practice. Specifically, we will entertain the notion that normative accounts play a very important practical role in journalism. In prior chapters, we learned that journalism is defined by constitutive rules about what the practice is and is for. In turn, these rules are anchored to broader constitutive commitments of public life. When journalists are asked to defend this or that practice, they inevitably appeal to these commitments. Such commitments therefore represent the crucial analytic link between journalism and the public. Here, I want to suggest that normative visions of journalism put these commitments in the conditional voice. That is, they constitute precisely the "repertoires of justification" (Lamont and Thévenot, 2000) to which journalists turn to justify their actions. Why did I do this, you ask? Well, because it is what I *should* do! Viewed this way, normative ideals about what journalism "should" or "could" be animate the emotions and direct the intentions of people who inhabit the field of journalism. These reservoirs of meaning infuse the journalistic imagination, shaping what it is we can imagine a journalist doing while still remaining within the realm of journalism. In short, values define the limits of what it is possible to do, and still remain within the boundaries of the field.

As we develop this idea, we should be aware that normative accounts of journalism are many and varied (Christians et al., 2009). Luckily, we have no need to go into the details of each of them. Instead, for our purposes we will organize them into three broad clusters. The first and most common is that journalism should tell the truth. By this observers may mean various things, among them: that journalism should be accurate; that it should be fair and/or impartial; that it should be independent and detached from the people and issues it covers; and that it should offer balanced, complete, and unbiased representations. These terms—"truth" and "objectivity," "fairness" and "impartiality," "bias" and "balance"—are not equivalent. Generally, though, they describe the idea that journalism ought to fashion accurate depictions of reality. A second vocabulary, not quite as longstanding, and not as common, is that the news should build community. Advocates of this view focus on questions like these: Do journalists represent all members of a community? Do they promote public participation? Do they manifest community values and mores? Do they cultivate civic virtue? Do they foster social capital? These terms—"diversity" and "representation," "public participation," "civic virtue," and "social capital"—comprise a vocabulary of community building. A third line of thinking, more recent than the others but perhaps more influential in the academic literature, claims that the news ought to be put to the service of a particular kind of community—a deliberative community. Journalism, this is to say, should catalyze considered public discussion of serious public issues. Here, "rationality" and "reason-giving," "information" and "deliberation," "talk" and "discussion," are common terms.

In reality, scholars often blend these vernaculars in their accounts of what journalism could or should be, but for descriptive purposes, we will treat each as an ideal type. In what follows, we sketch these normative traditions and then ask how they help to define the journalistic imagination.

The exercise allows us, I think, to make several observations about the imaginative resources available to journalists. A first is that truth-telling comprises the field's dominant vernacular. When journalists and others invested in journalism imagine what it should be, more often than not they imagine that, above all else, it should tell the truth. A second observation: journalism's collective imagination is strongly oriented to the state. Take the idea that journalism ought to tell the truth. Most often, journalists imagine this exercise in relation to the state. Even when they focus their attention elsewhere, they still rely on the state to verify the information they gather. This is not to say that community building is invisible in the field's collective imagination. Rather, it simply plays a minor role. In fact, it arises most often in conversations about journalism's role in political community, or the public sphere. This is a sphere that, as Habermas instructs us, arises in civil society but is *oriented to the state*. In other words, even when observers talk of journalism's role vis-à-vis building community, they often mean its relationship to the state.

A third observation follows. Journalism has a vexed relationship to market-based normative ideas for the field. In Anglo-America at least, there is a relatively strong market-based conception of *news*. It has to do with the metaphor of a "marketplace of ideas." According to this idea, information ought to circulate seamlessly, with little government interference, almost as if it exists in a free market, so that ideas may compete with one another on the basis of their merit. Beyond this image of news, there is far less support for a market-based conception of *journalism*. Even in Anglo-America, it is the rare journalist, or observer of journalism, who argues that journalism should be about the making of money. In fact, my survey of the literature has discovered only one: Schudson's (2005) contrarian argument that perhaps dependency on the market is not so bad for journalism. This isn't to say that the market is invisible. On occasion, one finds journalists appealing to the market as a way of insulating themselves from the state. An example is the relative enthusiasm for private ownership among American journalists. More broadly, the market tends to play a stronger role in the journalistic imagination as a foil or antagonist. Journalists generally view the market as a primary threat to their ideal images of what journalism could or should be. In playing this role, the market increases tension in the field—a tension, as we have explained in prior chapters, necessary for the field's integrity.

Given these contradictions, it is fair to say that no formal or systematic market-based normative vision for journalism exists. If there is any consistency it lies in journalists' general hostility to the market. The rest remains something of a grab bag of terms, deployed haphazardly across the field.

Overall, Blumler and Cushion have no need to worry about the fate of normative theory. It is a constituent part of the practice of journalism. Without it, journalists would be unable to figure out what it is possible to do while remaining within the confines of the field.

Normative Accounts

Imagine for a moment that you are a journalist-entrepreneur. Maybe you have a background in journalism. You might have worked at a newspaper, or a magazine, or a TV station. Or maybe you have no such background at all; you merely have an aspiration to be a writer and tell stories about your community. These days, cheap digital tools make starting your own news operation feasible. It is easy to create a website and get to work. But first you have to answer some basic questions. You want to be a journalist, but what does that mean? What will you actually *do* when you are doing journalism? Answers to this question presuppose answers to another: What can you *imagine* doing? What, in your mind, *should* a journalist do? Notice that you now find yourself in the conditional voice—the voice of would, could, and should. This is the voice of imagination, and it is this voice that infuses your emotions and informs your intentions as you set about making yourself into a digital journalist.

What do I mean when I say that the conditional voice infuses emotion and informs intention? I take the idea from Geertz (1973). In an essay on religion as a cultural system, Geertz (1973) defines religion as a system of symbols that "establishes . . . motivations in men by formulating conceptions of a general order of existence and clothing these conceptions with such an aura of factuality that the . . . motivations seem uniquely realistic" (p. 90). In this context, a motivation is a "tendency . . . to perform certain sorts of acts . . . in certain sorts of situations" (p. 96). To illustrate the point, Geertz takes from Ryle (1949) the example of a vain man. When we encounter a vain main, we expect that he will be self-regarding, that is, that he will focus most attention on himself, his pursuits, and his accomplishments. To be vain, Geertz writes, "is to tend to act in ways that are recognizably vain" (p. 96). Put another way, Geertz is saying that culture informs intention and produces passion. It engenders a willfulness or persistence enabling certain kinds of actions in the appropriate situations.

Journalism's conditional voice works in a similar way. Normative accounts order the symbolic environment in particular patterns. In so doing, they create the possibility of meaning, and so engender a willfulness to act. This process is as much social and cultural as it is individual. For anything you wish to do as a journalist you will have to justify to others who have investments in the practice (other journalists, members of the audience, and so on). This means that not only can you not do what you cannot imagine, you cannot recognizably do what *others* cannot imagine. In a sense, then, we might say that the conditional voice sketches the boundaries of journalism's collective imagination.

It is not surprising, therefore, that these accounts have existed since the beginnings of the field (Christians et al., 2009; Ward, 2004), or that they have deepened and multiplied ever since. Scholars have organized these accounts in different ways. In a recent review, for instance, Blumler and Cushion (2013) detect six traditions stretching back to the writings of John Dewey and Walter Lippmann. The six include discussions about journalism's role in different political systems, journalism's role in elections, obstacles to effective political communication, suitable journalistic roles and identities, the adequacy of political information conveyed in the news, and finally, journalism in the context of the good society, or the good political society. Others have clumped the normative literature in different ways (Christians et al., 2009). In my own reading, three basic propositions seem to underlie most of these normative accounts. Primary among these is that journalism, and journalists, should tell the truth. So let's begin there.

Journalism Should Tell the Truth

The idea that above all journalists should tell the truth is the most longstanding and pervasive normative understanding of journalism. Streckfuss (1990) notes that already in the 1600s John Milton used truth as a justification for freedom of publication. Similarly, Ward (2004) traces the advent of "proto-objectivity" in the news to the invention of weekly newssheets in seventeenth-century England (p. 90). According to Ward, publishers of these newssheets promoted themselves as chroniclers of facts. When we refer to uses of terms such as "facts" and "truth" we need to be careful. Words can have different meanings over time. For example, Nord (2001) observes that seventeenth-century Americans saw a need for truth in the news, but for them truth was "shaped by the belief that everything happened according to God's perfect plan" (p. 32). It was a religious truth that New Englanders sought, and they imagined a form of news that could detect and disseminate this truth. Nineteenth-century Americans also imagined that journalism should discover the truth. By this time, however, religion had ceded its primacy in public life to political parties. To these Americans, journalism should discover and represent a political truth, one rooted in a partisan view of the world. So while since its inception news production has been tasked with truth-seeking and fact-acquisition, what counts as truths worth seeking and facts worth acquiring varies.

Here, we will limit ourselves to the modern period—roughly from the 1920s forward. In this time, truth-telling has been associated with a basket of terms centered on the concept of objectivity. As we discussed in a prior chapter, this happened first and most decisively in the United States, where the profession first took root. American journalists began to use the word "objectivity" in the late 1920s (Streckfuss, 1990). However, as Maras (2013) notes, already in the 1830s a "proto-objectivity" had begun to pervade American journalism. By the 1870s and 1880s, the notion of journalism as a quasi science had taken hold (Schudson, 1978, p. 78; Schiller, 1981, p. 88). At this time, fledgling reporters began to imagine themselves as laying bare the underpinnings of society, much as scientists began to uncover the workings of nature. However, Streckfuss is in general right. It wasn't until the 1920s that objectivity became a professional norm within journalism, a "moral ideal," as Schudson (2001, p. 149) puts it, and a dominant "occupational value." It wasn't until the 1920s, in other words, that objectivity became a motivating force within the field.

The word "objectivity" is associated with a cluster of related terms (Mindich, 1998; Schudson, 2001). Partly it is a *philosophical attitude*: a preference for separating facts from values, a posture of detachment from events, and an impartial attitude. Objective journalists have no stake in the outcome of the events they cover. Partly objectivity is associated with an *ethic*, one of independence and fair play. An objective journalist maintains a distance from her sources, for instance, and strives above all to offer fair descriptions of events. She works, for example, to quote sources accurately, and to put those quotes in the proper context., and partly objectivity is linked to a set of *practices*, such as building stories out a tissue of gathered facts, verifying information, ensuring that points of view in news stories are balanced, or attributing facts to authoritative sources. Objective journalism is in this sense a method, one designed to discover more or less accurate approximations of the truth, or, as Kovach and Rosenstiel (2001) put it, "journalistic truth" (p. 42).

We might say that these words—facts from values, detachment and impartiality, facticity, balance, and attribution—comprise a repertoire of terms centered on objectivity that journalists and others deploy when discussing what journalists should do; they are the words journalists and others turn to when explaining why they do what they do, and why they should be doing it.

When we think of objectivity in this way, as a repertoire of justification, it is easy to see that the terms might be organized in different ways, that objectivity might mean slightly different things across societies, and in different positions in the field. Take, for instance, the case of advocacy journalists. There are many such people working in the field of journalism. As advocates, they clearly have stakes in outcomes. An environmental journalist cares deeply about the environment. A civil rights journalist sees herself as a champion of those rights. For this reason, advocacy journalists may think little of the notion that they should be detached from the issues they cover. They may not subscribe to the practice of balance, or distinguish between facts and values. Having admitted as much, they may still assert an interest in accuracy and in fact-based reporting. They may argue that the information they disseminate is based on facts, and has been verified via established journalistic practices. Within the repertoire of objectivity, in other words, they may stress fact gathering and verification and downplay values such as impartiality and practices like balance.

The same also is true cross-nationally. Many studies have shown that mainstream journalists in Western democracies embrace, more and less, some notion of objectivity (Weaver and Willnat, 2012). But European journalists see less need to make a strict separation between facts and values (Chalaby, 1996; Esser and Umbricht, 2014; Hampton, 2008; Høyer and Pöttker, 2005). Indeed, Italian journalists dispense nearly entirely with the practice of balance and attribution in their stories (Mancini, 2005). When one moves outside the Western context, the same holds. Most journalists everywhere embrace some notion of objectivity. But in Latin America journalists refuse a stance of impartiality (Waisbord, 2000), and in Asia objectivity is often associated with strong support for state actors (Hayashi, 2011; Maras and Nip, 2015; Zhao, 2012).

This is to say that the vocabulary associated with objectivity is flexible and malleable.

Despite this flexibility, objectivity is associated with professional journalism everywhere it is practiced. Why should this be true? Schudson (2001) offers four reasons. Two have to do with the internal needs of the profession. Objectivity is one way that journalists identify themselves to one another and create a kind of group solidarity. It is also a matter of external professional distinction: specifically, of distinguishing journalism from the host of other professional communicators (public relations professionals, advertising professionals, political professionals) who populate the public sphere. Journalism is unique, the argument goes, because it strives to produce objective reports. Two other reasons for the prevalence of objectivity have to do with external social control. Objectivity is a way for editors and publishers to exert control over what are often large and unwieldy newsrooms. Editors can demand that journalists adhere to particular values and practices., and publishers can insist that journalists remain objective so that they avoid politically contentious issues.

Not all of these conditions matter, or matter as much, in each context. But at least some do in every context. Together, they have made the vocabulary of objectivity central to the field's self-conception.

As such, objectivity has been incredibly productive for the field. I mean by this that it has catalyzed a nearly constant stream of conversation about whether and how journalists are, should be, or could be objective. This conversation began with Lippmann's (1922) assertion that journalists should strive to tell the truth, and that they might rely on "political observatories," that is, state agencies, to help them do so. Since then, it has only grown louder. Beginning in the 1970s, critics began to mount a vigorous assault on the ideal of objectivity. Some argued that an objective view is epistemologically impossible (Altheide, 1976; Durham, 1998). Others pointed out that, in practice, objective journalism unduly tied journalism to the state (Bennett, 1983). What does an objective journalist do, after all, but gather facts from one institutional choice and verify them through appeal to another? At best, the close proximity in which objectivity places journalism to the state leaves the field, others argue, intellectually neutered (Glasser, 1992). Journalism, on this view, becomes little more than a technical exercise. At worse, objectivity becomes a "strategic ritual" (Tuchman, 1972), a shield journalists use to defend themselves against their critics.

These criticisms have had their effect on the field (Bell, 1998; Overholser, 2006), and dampened use of the term "objectivity." But the critics have not dislodged objectivity from its pride of place. Even today, after decades of criticism, truth-telling in the guise of objectivity remains a powerful ideal for journalists. In an age of spin and "truthiness," they defend its epistemological value (Fuller, 1996; Scheuer, 2008). They develop new philosophical defenses of the term rooted in realist or pragmatic philosophy (Figdor, 2010; Muñoz-Torres, 2012; Ward, 2004). They argue that objectivity is less an ideal than a method, and then defend those methods as basic to good journalism (Kovach and Rosenstiel, 2001). They replace use of the term with new ones, like "impartiality," "fairness," "accuracy," and most recently, "transparency." Above all, they defend the idea that journalism is, and ought to be, a truth-seeking exercise. If journalism isn't after the truth, they ask, what is it for?

Journalism Should Build Community

When the trappings of modernity (such as industrialization, urbanization, and secularism) emerged in the 1800s, observers began to assign a new role to journalism. Hegel was one of the first to hint at this role in an enigmatic comment written in one of his notebooks sometime between 1803 and 1805. "Reading the newspaper," Buck-Morss (2000, p. 844) quotes him as writing, "is a kind of realistic morning prayer. [In newspaper reading] one orients one's attitude toward that which the world is." Here, Hegel suggests that newspapers are replacing a traditional institution—religion—in helping people understand and navigate the world around them.

Hegel never followed up on his intriguing comment, but

two decades later, using slightly different language, Alexis de Tocqueville did. On his visit to America in 1831, Tocqueville was struck by the role of associations in democratic society. "Better use has been made of associations," he writes, "and this powerful instrument of action has been applied to more varied aims in America than in anywhere in the world" (1840/1969, p. 189). Why were associations so vital in the United States? Part of their use, Tocqueville surmised, was as a hedge against any individual or small group from assuming absolute political power. Tocqueville also saw that, in a modern society characterized by more individual freedom and fewer traditional ties, associations allow individuals to coordinate collective action and express common values. That is why "at the head of any new undertaking," he writes, "where in France you would find the government or in England some territorial magnate, in the United States you are sure to find an association" (p. 513).

Just as associations are vital to democratic life, newspapers, Tocqueville surmises, are central to associations. On the one hand, newspapers are the only effective means to "put the same thought at the same time before [a mass] of readers" (p. 517). In this sense, they are a tool for organizing and coordinating groups. On the other hand, they are a means for transmitting values. "A newspaper can only survive," Tocqueville observes, "if it gives publicity to feelings or principles common to a large number of men" (p. 519). In a society with few collective ties, newspapers are vital for the creation and maintenance of community. Translating Tocqueville's thought into Hegel's terms, we might say that newspaper reading had become part of America's civil religion.

Made at the cusp of modernity, when the impact of urbanization and industrialization on traditional society was only dimly perceived, Hegel and Tocqueville's insights were startling. As time passed, however, observers returned to these thoughts again and again. In 1887, for instance, Tönnies (1887/1957) argued that traditional community (*gemeinschaft*) was fast giving way to modern society (*gesselschaft*). Like Hegel and Tocqueville, Tönnies saw that society (as opposed to community) was organized on different principles. For one thing, public opinion rather than the church now oriented people to the world. And, of course, he saw the press as central to public opinion: "the press is the real instrument . . . of public opinion. . . . It is comparable and, in some respects, superior to the material power which the states possess through their armies, their treasuries, and their bureaucratic civil service" (p. 221). Robert Park's (1922) work on the American immigrant press is another example. "Immigrants," he observed, "organize," and news is central to this practice: "news is a kind of urgent information that men use in making adjustments to a new environment, in changing old habits and in forming new opinions" (p. 9).

No one made the connection between news, community, and modern public life more famously than John Dewey. Dewey was spurred to write on the subject by Walter Lippmann, who, in a series of books, argued that the "public is a phantom" and democracy as historically understood is, in modern society, impossible (1922, 1925). In a review of this work, Dewey called it "perhaps the most effective indictment of democracy as currently conceived ever penned" (Dewey, 1922, p. 286). Was Lippmann right and democracy simply impossible in modern society? In *The Public and Its Problems* (1927), Dewey argued that Lippmann was wrong. The public is not a "phantom," he stated, it is merely disorganized (p. 109). "The machine age has so enormously expanded, multiplied, intensified and complicated the scope [of society] . . . have formed such immense and consolidated unions in action, on an impersonal rather than a community basis, that the resultant public cannot identify and distinguish itself" (p. 126). This is Dewey's diagnosis. His cure? In a word, communication. "We have the physical tools of communication [at our disposal]. . . . Without such communication the public will remain shadowy and formless. . . Till the Great Society is converted into a Great Community, the Public will remain in eclipse" (p. 142).

When Dewey imagined the "new tools of communication," he thought of movies and advertising, broadcasting and public relations. Most of all, however, he thought of the news. Not the fragmentary news of gossip and sensation that was (and remains) the daily grist of news, however; rather, Dewey imagined a deliberative and rational form of news, one that organized and reported the results of scientific (or at least administrative) inquiries. Modern social sciences provided a structure for such inquiry. Dewey surmised that a way was needed to turn these technical and abstract inquiries into effective communication for citizens. He found his solution in the news. To him, news promised to bring scientific inquiries to ground, to make them real, timely, and relevant.

In his response to Lippmann, Dewey crystallized the long line of thought stretching back to Hegel: journalism, he imagined, might animate a "Great Community," a community fit for the modern age. This image of journalism swept through the field, especially in the second half of the twentieth century. According to one source, the first "community journalism" course was offered at the University of North Carolina in 1961 (Lauterer, 2006, p. xviii). Since then, the image of journalism as a community builder has persisted within the profession (Forde, 2011; Reader and Hatcher, 2012).

Like objectivity, the phrase "community journalism" has mushroomed into a web of semantic associations. The most common association made is between community and geographic size. Community journalism, the thought goes, takes place in villages and neighborhoods, small towns and rural areas. It is, as Lauterer (2006) puts it in the title of his book on the subject, "relentlessly local." In developing countries, community journalism is sometimes linked to economic sustainability, or so-called development journalism (Bowd, 2006; Maslog, 1985, 1989; Moore and Gillis, 2005). Community journalism is often linked to civic participation: the more community news, the thought goes, the more civic participation. Researchers sometimes formalize this relationship in the term "social capital," a kind of resource citizens and communities may produce and accrue to foster greater social cooperation (Putnam, 1995). A different association is one between community and nation. The news connects people to so-called imagined communities, as Anderson (1983) refers to them, or broad conceptions of nationhood. In each of these connections, the idea is that journalism produces and reproduces symbols that tie people to one another. Shared symbolic environments create conditions for higher rates of civic activity and social cooperation.

Scholars have shown this theory to have some basis in reality. Much of the research on community journalism has been conducted in the US. Ironically, it has been inspired less by a concern for revamping community than for increasing newspaper readership. Faced with declining circulations, the newspaper industry in the 1960s began to fund research on the question of why people read (or do not read) the news. Morris Janowitz (1957, p. 12)—a student of Park's—provided an early answer when he found that individuals who were more integrated into their communities were more likely to read the newspaper (see also Merton, 1950). Community ties, that is, correlate with news consumption. Since Janowitz's work, dozens of studies have confirmed this relationship (see Stamm, 1985, for an interim review; Mersey, 2010, for a more recent review). Researchers have defined a community tie in different ways—in terms of participation and political knowledge, belonging to civic groups and family history (Lowrey et al., 2008). Some have substituted the term "social capital" for "community tie," to ask whether and the extent to which news consumption promotes the creation of social capital (Putnam, 2000; Richards, 2012)., and they have defined journalism differently as well, making a distinction, for instance, between television consumption and newspaper reading (Jeffres et al., 1988). They have never been able to show whether it is news consumption that prompts community ties or the other way around. They have demonstrated a correlation between the two, however. If an individual consumes news habitually, he or she is more likely to be politically knowledgeable and civically involved. In short: more news = stronger community (and vice versa).

Despite all the attention to the ideal of community journalism, its practice has never gained a great following within the field, certainly as compared to its concern to tell the truth. This is so for two reasons, both of which involve the self-conception of journalism as a profession, and both of which were identified by the early writings. The first is that community news (as opposed to state-oriented news) tends to focus on gossip more than on serious (read: governmental) matters. Park (1922), for example, remarks of the immigrant press that it contains mostly gossip and few genuine ideas (p. 70)., and Dewey concedes that stories of "crime, accident, family rows, personal clashes and conflicts" fill the daily newspaper. This fact makes it "sound ridiculous," he writes, "to say that a genuine social science [might] manifest its reality in the daily press" (p. 180). Why are community newspapers especially prone to frivolous news? Part of the reason has to do with the audience. As Park observes, people *like* to hear gossip, especially about their neighbors (see also Shibutani, 1966)., and part of it has to do with the fact that news organizations are for-profit enterprises. It is in their economic interest, after all, to give audiences precisely what they like and not necessarily what they need (Bagdikian, 1983; Baker, 2002). Moreover, it is cheaper to do so, and requires less professional skill. Whatever the reason, journalists tend to privilege serious, state-oriented, hard news over the more playful, community-oriented, soft news of the community newspaper.

The other reason that community journalism is less prominent in the field has to do with political power. It did not escape the attention of Dewey, Park, and other early observers that editors and publishers of community newspapers were prominent men in their communities. Such men had personal and professional ties to the major businesses in their communities, and to political and civic leaders. So when their newspapers did produce more serious news, it tended to be framed in terms of the points of views of the most powerful members of the community; it tended to privilege consensus rather than conflict—to express, that is, dominant community values; and, to this extent, it tended to ignore the views, interests, and needs of less powerful community members. Writing of Chicago's community press in the 1950s, Janowitz observes that the "community press acts as a mechanism which seeks to maintain consensus through the emphasis on common values rather than on the solution of conflicting values" (p. 60). Others have demonstrated that community-oriented news tilts toward consensus rather than conflict (Tichenor et al., 1980).

Over time, these facts generated a sense among many in the field that community-oriented news was less professional than state-oriented news. In the first instance, it was seen as requiring less skill to write a "softer" form of journalism. Entry-level journalists often obtained their first jobs at community-oriented small town newspapers, or less often as staff writers for the community section of a larger regional newspaper. It was here that they learned the basics of journalism, and it was from here that they hoped to graduate to more serious and prestigious newspapers or beats. In the second, it implicated journalists in the communities they covered in ways they found uncomfortable. Community-oriented journalism was viewed as overly value-laden, and even as "boosterism" or cheerleading for the dominant political, economic, and value structure (Kaniss, 1991).

Many journalists disagreed (and continue to disagree) with these assessments, but they have stuck., and so the vernacular of community journalism—participation and civic-mindedness, public knowledge and community action, sustainability and development—remains an important yet minor part of the journalistic imagination.

Journalism Should Foster Deliberative Conversation

Implicit in Tocqueville's ruminations on democratic associations, and Dewey's interest in the Great Community, is the issue of political talk. Consider the situation. Modern society is larger and more complex than traditional society, and modern individuals are more isolated and autonomous from one another. Yet, in a democracy we imagine that citizens (should) participate in collective decisions, which must mean, at some level, that they have opportunities to talk to one another. But how are these conversations supposed to happen? Why would citizens be motivated to engage with people they do not know around problems that seem insurmountable? Who would facilitate these conversations? And how would they scale from face-to-face to societal discussions?

In writings that stretch back to the 1960s, Jurgen Habermas (1989, 1996) has focused new attention on these questions. It is not an exaggeration to say that his work has catalyzed an entire field of study. In the earliest of this work, Habermas examines the early modern bourgeois public sphere. It was here, Habermas argues, that early modern Europeans invented new "institutions of publicity." Salons and coffeehouses, taverns and newspapers—these institutions fostered a peculiar form of *talk*: of conversation, discussion, and debate. Borrowing from Kant, Habermas sometimes calls this talk the "public use of reason"; within his theory of modern society, he also refers to it as "communicative rationality." Others have taken to calling it, more simply, public deliberation. Habermas argues that public deliberation depends upon well-functioning institutions of publicity that operate in a *public sphere*: a sphere of civil society oriented to the state (on other models of the public sphere, see Ferree et al., 2002).

Habermas's story about the rise of the bourgeois public sphere has been ably summarized elsewhere (Calhoun, 1992, and others). In outline, however, the story is this: in the middle ages, publicness in Europe was little more than representativeness, in the sense that the monarchy embodied (or represented) the public. Wherever the monarch went, so went the public. This began to change in the seventeenth and eighteenth centuries, a time when heightened commercial activity allowed the formation of a new middle-class or bourgeois society. Relatively independent from the state, and more cosmopolitan and literate, the individuals in this social stratum began to interact in new social spaces—in salons and coffee houses, taverns and theaters—and in newspapers. Habermas argues that these "institutions of publicity" formed a separate "public sphere," a social space between the state and the market. In these spaces, bourgeois citizens created a new kind of social intercourse, one that combined equality and inclusiveness with rationality and argument. Modeled first in the arts and sciences (Ezrahi, 1990) and religion (Zaret, 2000), this mode of interaction, what we may call public deliberation, eventually migrated to the world of politics. As this happened, the political talk that took place in the public sphere became a kind of steering mechanism for the state. In short, it was through the public sphere that early modern citizens solved the conundrum of how democratic conversations might take place in modern societies.

In the second part of his book, Habermas famously details the decline of the bourgeois public sphere during the nineteenth century, mostly at the hands of the market and the rise of the administrative state. Mass media play a central role in this tale. To Habermas, commercial mass media do not serve as a forum for public debate. Instead, they package discourse into formulas (like the lede paragraph, or the balanced news story). Moreover, policymakers take advantage of these formulas to press their views on a relatively passive, consumerist public. In the process, arguments are no longer waged in public space. Instead, they are merely represented, as in the middle ages, rehearsed for a public that has been relegated to the margins of public life. In the event, the public use of reason has dissipated, and the public sphere has become little more than "a vehicle for political and economic propaganda" (p. 175).

Habermas made this argument in the early 1960s, but it wasn't until 1989 that the book appeared in English. Immediately, it sparked an explosive response among academics. Just one journal, *Media, Culture & Society*, published nearly sixty articles on the public sphere in the decade between 1990 and 2000, and has published nearly 350 articles to date (Lunt and Livingstone, 2013, p. 87)! Little of this work has taken Habermas's conception at face value. Habermas's critics have complained that he mischaracterizes the early bourgeois public sphere as overly rational and disembodied (Baker, 1990; Eley, 1994; Ryan, 1990). Emotion, they argue, is every bit as important to public discourse as reason, even in the heyday of the bourgeois public sphere. They observe that his description of rational talk privileges white, masculine forms of discourse (Young, 1990). They note that there has never been just one public sphere, but many (Fraser, 1990). Subordinate groups, including the working classes, women, and people of color, have created many of these "counter-publics," as Warner (2002) calls them, to directly confront the dominant mode of public discourse (see also Negt and Kluge, 1993).

In later work, Habermas (1996) incorporated many of these criticisms into his model of the public sphere. However, his conception of deliberative talk has remained consistent over time. To him, deliberative talk requires that everyone have an opportunity to participate in conversations (an equality criterion). It requires that information circulated should represent the diversity of views in a community (a diversity criterion), and, most important, that public conversations ought to be based in the public use of reason (a deliberation criterion). Habermas means by this that public talk requires people to give reasons for their views, and these reasons should be oriented to persuading others of the claim; in turn, listeners should incorporate the reasons of others into their own views (a reciprocity criterion); and finally, deliberative conversations should serve as a steering mechanism for the exercise of legislative power (a political criterion). Even today, these ideal conditions serve as a normative benchmark against which observers assess the democratic performance of actually existing media systems. As Habermas (1996) puts it, "these principles express a simple idea: the mass media ought to understand themselves as the mandatory of an enlightened public whose willingness to learn and capacity for criticism they at once presuppose, demand and reinforce" (p. 378).

The influence of Habermas's theory is fed by many factors. In part it is due to the fact that he built his model on top of a long history of thinking on the role of civil society in public life (Somers, 1995). Partly, it is a matter of timing. The English translation of Habermas's work came at a time of increasing worry in Europe and the U.S. about the increasing intrusion of markets further into public life. In Europe, for example, Habermas helped scholars think about the fate of public service broadcasting in an era of deregulation (Born, 2003; Curran, 1991; Dawes, 2014; Garnham, 1993; Keane, 1991; Lunt and Livingstone, 2013; Scannell, 1989). After the fall of the Berlin Wall, Habermas's story of the public sphere also opened a space for thinking about how media might contribute to a reconstituted public life in the former communist states. In the United States, observers had been worrying about the "commercialization" of the news industry for at least the previous decade (McManus, 1994; Underwood, 1993). Habermas's work provided a frame for many of these criticisms (Hallin, 1994). Later, in the 2000s, interest in the public sphere in Europe turned toward the prospects for the formation of a transnational European public sphere (Fossum and Schlesinger, 2007;

Risse, 2010; Koopmans and Statham, 2010). This work has kept the public sphere at the center of conversations about the relation of media to democracy.

The notion that journalism ought to contribute to a vibrant public sphere is today widely accepted (Ettema, 2007; Dahlgren and Sparks, 1991; McNair, 2000). Whether conducting research on journalism's contribution to the American or European public sphere, most scholars simply assume that this sphere can and should exist (Nitoiu, 2013). The notion, after all, seems commonsensical. Democracy requires collective decision-making; ostensibly, these decisions should be grounded in a public use of reason; these reasons ought to be available to everyone; and journalism (more broadly, media) is the only institution capable of serving as a forum for a public debate that meets these criteria.

Despite its wide following, the empirical literature has not been kind to this consensus. It may be conventional wisdom that journalism *should* contribute to the public sphere, but the reality, many studies confirm, is that, most of the time, it does not—at least as measured by metrics like inclusiveness, equality, participation, reciprocity, and reason-giving. Consider, for instance, the literature that has arisen on the possibilities for a European public sphere. Study after study has shown that most national media are resolutely nationalist in orientation (e.g., Preston, 2009; Schlesinger, 1999). In other words, they rarely air transnational issues, and so violate the criteria of inclusiveness. When Europe-wide issues do appear in the pages of newspapers, journalists tend to rely on elite sources to write about them, a violation of the participation criterion (Risse, 2010; Schlesinger, 1999). Some observers have noted that, in recent years, transnational media such as Euronews have emerged (Brüggemann and Schulz-Forberg, 2009; Garcia-Blanco and Cushion, 2010). These media may herald the dawn of pan-European identity (Olausson, 2010). To date, however, these organizations have attracted relatively small, narrow, and elite audiences (again, violating the norms of inclusiveness and participation). In short, on the available evidence, European journalism has yet to contribute much to the formation of a European public sphere.

A similar story can be told of American journalism. Patterson (1992) shows that when covering political campaigns journalists mostly focus on the horse race, a kind of coverage that violates the criterion of public reason. Scholars have been especially critical of television (Capella and Jamieson, 1997; Hallin, 1994; Iyengar, 1994; Iyengar and Kinder, 1989; Moy and Gastil, 2006). Not only does TV news frame issues in ways that inhibit deep political learning, it also reduces overall political participation. That is, the more TV news citizens watch, the less likely they are to participate in public life. On these measures, print news does a bit better. Individuals who read the newspaper are more likely to participate in public life, and to be more knowledgeable about politics. Yet, like TV news, the daily grist of newspaper journalism tends to offer a fragmented, sensationalized, and personalized view of the political world. This inhibits public deliberation (Bennett, 1983). For reasons we have discussed elsewhere, journalism also privileges elite opinion, a fact that limits the diversity of views in the public sphere (Entman, 1989; Page, 1996).

In short, if Habermas's conception of the public sphere is the benchmark, it appears that journalism largely fails to live up to its democratic obligations (Jacobs and Townsley, 2011). To some critics (Zelizer, 2012), the obvious gap between *is* and *ought* indicates that perhaps we should reimagine the benchmark. Perhaps, in other words, we ought to view journalism through something other than the prism of public deliberation and the public sphere. Zelizer (2012) argues just this, and blames a "western-driven and universal standard of subjunctive action" (p. 468) for the resilience of the vernacular. Despite these protests, and despite the empirical evidence, however, the vernacular has stuck. Especially among academics—deliberation and reason giving, equality and participation—remain vital concepts for imagining what journalism should or could be.

Journalists themselves have been more equivocal. In the 1980s and 1990s, a movement inspired by the ideal of public deliberation, alternately called public or civic journalism, arose within the field. It mostly found a home at small and midsized daily newspapers, and mostly in the United States. By 2002, however, more than 600 public journalism experiments had been launched (Friedland and Nichols, 2002), and more than a few of these experiments took place at larger news outlets, and in Europe and Latin America. Surveying the scene at the time, Schudson (1999) called public journalism the "most impressive critique of journalistic practice inside journalism in a generation" (p. 118).

Loosely coordinated, and stretched across many newsrooms, public journalists never developed a coherent alternative vision for their field, which is not surprising. It is fair to say, however, that a primary goal, shared across most experiments, was to stimulate more public deliberation (Haas, 2007, Chap. 2). For instance, the Minneapolis *Star Tribune* initiated a series of "Minnesota's Talking" roundtables in which citizens engaged in small-group facilitated conversations about public issues. Similarly, the Wisconsin *State Journal* collaborated with Wisconsin Public Radio and TV to hold a "We the People" event that involved citizens in televised deliberations. Overall, more than half of the 600 experiments catalogued by Friedland and Nichols (2002) included a public deliberation component.

This activity demonstrates that the vernacular of the public sphere gained currency in the field. That currency is limited, however, as demonstrated by the reaction of other journalists to public journalism. Almost immediately, public journalism met a groundswell of criticism within the field (Haas, 2007, Chap. 4). Many journalists were uncomfortable with the almost religious zeal of public journalism's practitioners. They accused public journalists of being "true believers," of "preaching a gospel of salvation" for journalism. This stood in contrast to the longstanding notion that good journalists should be, above all, objective, independent, and detached.

More were uncomfortable with what they took to be public journalism's orientation to the market. Critics argued that, in focusing so much attention on *talk*, public journalists failed to recognize commercialism as *the* fundamental threat to "good journalism." On this view, public journalists did not resist the market strongly enough, did not fight against its interference with enough conviction. Other critics accused public journalism of being a marketing ploy itself. As Haas (2007) puts it, "to many journalists, public journalism [was] not merely likely to serve the circulation and profit interests of media owners and advertisers; it [was], in fact, a deliberate, corporate strategy embraced by managements to advance commercial concerns" (p. 70). What was their evidence? Critics pointed to the fact that public journalists focused much more attention on audiences than on state institutions—just as the "bean counters" on the business side of newsrooms desired. Moreover, the conversational forums favored by public journalists smacked of focus groups. Good journalists did not have to ask audiences what they wanted or needed in the news. As professionals, they knew what good journalism was, and they were intent on doing it regardless of what audiences wanted. The very fact that many editors and publishers were in favor of it was enough for many journalists to become hostile to public journalism. None of this evidence was definitive. But it was enough to kill the movement. By the early 2000s, public journalism was, for all intents and purposes, dead (Nip, 2006). The foundations that supported it had moved on, as had the scholars who wrote about it. Its leaders among journalists either died or were drummed out of the field.

The rise of public journalism shows that the vernacular of the public sphere has had an impact on the field. But its death demonstrates that journalists have been more equivocal about those ideals than scholars. The story of public journalism illuminates something else. It shows just how hostile journalists are to anything that smacks of commercialism. Within the field, the easiest way to generate opposition to a new practice is to say that it is commercially motivated. This wariness began long ago, during the field's formation in the early twentieth century. Let's end by placing this observation in the broader context of the journalistic imagination.

What Should Journalists Do?

We began this exercise with a thought experiment. Place yourself once again in the position of a journalist-entrepreneur. You want to do journalism, but it is only possible to do what one can imagine doing. So what is it that you can imagine doing, and still be recognizable as a journalist?

When we think of answers to this question, one obvious conclusion comes to mind: telling the truth is the most longstanding, the most obvious, and the most deeply motivating statement in the journalistic imagination. Walter Lippmann's suggestion that "there can be no higher law in journalism than to tell the truth" is broadly accepted in the field. Just to give one example: when Kovach and Rosenstiel (2001) surveyed journalists to better understand the "elements" that are central to journalism, one hundred percent(!) of respondents said that journalists should "tell the truth." The authors made this the subject of their first chapter.

Community building lies within the horizon of journalism's vision, though more faintly than truth-telling. In the U.S., it is most visible in small-town journalism, publications typically more dedicated to advancing the community than exposing state action. It is also expressed in the "development journalism" practiced in some developing countries, such as Thailand or Brazil. Generally, the vernacular of community building becomes most visible when it is defined in terms of the public sphere (or political society). It is there, where community building links to the state, that it animates the work of more journalists, and gains more prestige within the field. But nowhere is community building more motivating for journalists than truth-telling.

This is not to say, by the way, that community building is at odds with truth-telling, or that in reality they are not intermingled. It is possible to tell the truth and build community at the same time. It is to say, however, that as ideals the two are not the same. They imply different orientations to yourself, your work, and the publics you serve. As one example, a journalist oriented to the truth will strive for detachment. If truth is the goal, it will not do to get too close to one's sources or one's audience. In contrast, a community-oriented journalist necessarily will be *attached* to the communities she serves. Her passions are those of her community. A community journalist does what is best for the community, whether it involves holding government accountable or not. When journalists combine the vernaculars, they must negotiate these cross-cutting pressures.

Promotion of public sphere values is one place where those pressures might be felt. This vernacular orients journalists toward politics, and so brings them close to matters of state, and to values of truth-telling. Yet, as an exercise in community building, the public sphere places journalists in civil society among citizens, and so orients them to values of community building. In a truth-telling mode, journalists ferret out the truth, disseminate it, and consider this a job well done. Not so for journalists dedicated to their public sphere. They consider it their duty to ensure that citizens talk about the issues raised by the truth. They may go so far as to facilitate these conversations, and lead the community to collective decisions. The subsequent pushing and pulling may cause friction, as evidenced by the controversy that surrounded public journalism.

A second observation follows: journalism's inclination toward truth-telling shades the field's vision toward the state (see Figure 4.1). It isn't that civil society, political society, and the market have no purview in the field. It is just that they are marginal to the field's collective vision, especially when compared to the state. As journalists strive to tell the truth, the state looms large in their imaginations—for two reasons. First, as Lippmann recognized nearly one hundred years ago, reporters must turn to state agencies when they seek out the truth. Where else, for instance, can

Figure 4.1 Journalism's Collective Vision

127

a reporter turn to verify facts about crime other than the court-house and the police department? Journalistic truth-telling is an institutional exercise, and most of the relevant institutions reside within the state (Graves, 2016)., and second, when journalists imagine telling the truth, they do so most often in the context of the state, or political power generally. Think of a few of the now-hackneyed conceptions that have circulated in the field for decades. Journalism "speaks truth to power," it "afflicts the comfortable and comforts the afflicted," and it "shines a light in dark places." They are hackneyed because they are so common. The highest ideal within journalism is to hold government account-able, which within the field means to reveal the truth about what government does, is doing, or wishes to do. No practice has more prestige within the field.

This brings us to a third observation: the market plays a peculiar role within the collective imagination of the field. In general, the market lies at the margins of the field's vision. It is a rare journalist who is in it for the money. At the same time, the market is a topic of constant conversation in the field but the role it plays varies across society and context. In Anglo-America, a market-based rhetoric is sometimes deployed to insulate journalism from inter-ference by the state. For example, when then-Senator John Kerry held hearings in 2009 on the future of journalism, his committee openly considered public subsidies of the press. Many journalists blanched at this idea, preferring the protection of private owner-ship from interference by the state. More generally, however, it is fair to say that the market often plays the role of foil, or antago-nist, to "good journalism." Always in the background, the market offers a necessary contrast to make preferred values (like truth-telling) more apparent.

Debates around public journalism are one example of this phenomenon. Another is the policy literature that has built up in conversations about media regulation. For decades, policymakers and others have debated how to craft policies to give incentives, or even outright require, journalism to uphold its democratic com-mitments (Baker, 2002; Freedman, 2008; Lunt and Livingstone, 2013; Sunstein, 1995). Consider for a moment how this literature has been framed. In the U.K., Nicholas Garnham (1983) set the terms of a debate in the early 1980s with an essay titled "Public Service versus the Market" (Collins, 1993). Ever since, British scholars have argued over the extent to which (but not whether) markets are destructive of a vibrant British public sphere (Lunt and Livingstone, 2013). Similarly, in the United States, a long line of thinking exists on the need to shield journalism from markets. For instance, Baker (1994) recommends a relaxed interpretation of the press clause of the First Amendment, thus allowing government to intervene more strongly to, for instance, increase the diversity of media owners., and Sunstein (1995) argues that a purely market-based interpretation of the public sphere violates the spirit, if not the letter, of the First Amendment. Within these conversations, markets typically are cast as the foil of good public policy. It is true that in recent years scholars have softened, and complicated, their attack on markets (Dawes, 2014; Hesmondhalgh and Toynbee, 2008). But the general point holds. Even today, scholars tend to pit neoliberalism (or the logic of the market) against the needs of the public sphere (Harrison and Woods, 2001).

These examples demonstrate that the market plays a complicated role in journalism's collective imagination. Sometimes, especially in Anglo-America, it is mobilized to argue against state inference. More often, the market is taken to form the necessary background against which other ideals are put forward in the field. Truth-telling can only take place, journalists argue, when they are allowed to do their jobs free of interference from commercial imperatives. Similarly, arguments in favor of community-based journalism are often cast in opposition to market-based principles.

Noting as much provides a segue to the next chapter. As we have learned, modern journalism has been built out of the collective imagination of generations of journalists. The "repertoires of justification" we have discussed fuel this imagination. They motivate and inspire, inform and catalyze. This is even true of the market. Cast as an ever-present threat, it animates and catalyzes journalists every bit as much as their more positive ideals. All of these vernaculars contribute to the symbolic stuff that journalists use to turn their ideals into reality. Blumler and Cushion (2013) should have no fear, therefore, that normative theory is being marginalized, in journalism or in journalism studies.

What happens, however, when conditions change, and a key vernacular no longer resonates so well? This is one way of describing what has transpired with the advent of digital journalism. Simply put, no one has figured out a business model for digital news, at least one that can support a newsroom of the scale that existed in a print world (Levy and Nielsen, 2010). This fact has caused unprecedented misery in the field. In the United States, news organizations have failed, and thousands of journalists have lost their jobs. The situation is not so dire elsewhere but journalists throughout Europe nonetheless also feel their field to be in crisis (Nielsen, 2016a). These trends raise a new question: what happens when journalism's longstanding foil goes away? For generations, journalists fired their imaginations in part by fighting the forces of excess commercialism. Yet, today, it is the *loss* of commercialism that represents an existential threat to the field. How are journalists responding to this reversal?

This is the subject of Chapter Five.

5

Journalism and Change

Depending upon whom you read, journalism today is being disrupted (Nieman Reports, 2012), rebuilt (Anderson, 2013), reconstructed (Downie and Schudson, 2010), rethought (Peters and Broersma, 2013) and/or reconsidered (Alexander et al., 2016). Everyone agrees that it is changing (Anderson et al., 2012). There is little agreement about what this means. Is *all* of journalism changing, or only the way it pays for itself? What is causing journalism to change? Technology? Economics? Politics? When did the change begin? The 1990s? The 1960s? Earlier? Some observers believe the end of journalism is at hand (Charles and Stewart, 2011). "Will the last journalist," McChesney and Picard (2011) ask, "turn out the lights?" Others agree with Downie and Schudson (2010) that there is "abundant opportunity in the future of journalism." There is no topic that attracts more attention in the field today, and none that causes more confusion and disagreement, than change.

In this chapter, we place the question of change in the context of all that we have learned in prior chapters about the relationship between journalism and public life. Doing so will not resolve all the issues raised by ongoing debates, but it will bring clarity to a few central issues. One has to do with the very definition of the term. What, precisely, does it mean to say that journalism, or some aspect of it, is *changing*? A second theme has to do with time. Different changes may happen along different timelines (some shorter, some longer). Moreover, different forces, internal and external to the field, may be responsible for these changes. A third theme has to do with space. Not only may different changes happen at different times, but change may mean something different across geography as well. For instance, the same change may mean something different in Scandinavia than it does in Anglo-America; in Latin America it may be different than in Asia. When we say that journalism is undergoing "disruption" or "revolution," or is being "rethought" or "reconsidered," we should be careful to specify *where* we think this is happening. Finally, a last theme has to do with persistence. As we delve into these issues it will become clear that many aspects of journalism are not changing. We won't understand change very well if we cannot also explain how and why key elements of journalism remain durable and constant.

These are our themes, then, as we think about change in journalism. In what follows, we will take a tour through the ongoing conversation about journalism and change, focusing intently on the themes above. Since we'll do so using the tools and concepts we have developed in prior chapters, we will start with a brief recap.

A Recap

In prior chapters, we learned that modern journalism inflated as an occupational field first in the United States and later in other parts of the West. It emerged out of friction created by the tension between the state, the market, and the emergent profession. For convenience, I have reproduced Figure 2.3 below (that for consistency's sake, I have labeled Figure 5.1). As it shows, all three of the forces shown were important to the rise of journalism, but the *relationship* between them was vital. I used the metaphor of a tent to illustrate this process. Much as a tent rises when its poles push and pull against one another, so journalism inflated in the pushing and pulling among the state, the market, and the profession. Journalism's distinctive properties (that is, detachment, independence, facticity, the inverted pyramid style of writing) are ways that

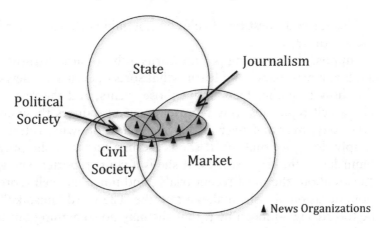

Figure 5.1   The Journalistic Field in the United States

journalists came to manage their complicated existence, pulled in the one direction by their sources (mostly public officials), in another by the imperatives of the market, and in still another by the demands of their own profession.

Within the newly emergent field, journalism became more organized and ordered. It developed preferred identities, values, and patterns of behaviors. Walk into any newsroom and you will find journalists producing news in a more or less organized, consistent way. To produce a story, they do this, and then this, and then this. We have called these patterns institutionalized rules, and it is these rules that distinguish journalism from other social fields such as practicing law or giving a lecture or policing a community. It is important that the rules of journalism have not been codified, agreed upon, and formalized. Textbooks exist, of course, but they are filled with examples, not formal rules. Mostly this is because no particular rendition of a rule can account for every case. Such rules would be inadequate to the messy world in which journalists ply their trade. So journalists are left to learn the rules by example. That is, they are shown how to perform an action—how to gather facts, for example, or how to write a news lede, and then are asked to generalize from these examples to other instances. The rules of journalism, in this sense, do not precede action. Instead, journalists learn the rules simply by doing journalism.

This raises a question: if rules do not guide behavior, then what use are they?

Suppose that a young person learns to be a journalist: she takes a job at a newspaper and learns what sorts of events are newsworthy, how to gather facts about those events, and the rest. Much like a cell replicates, this reporter then reproduces these actions every day, over and over again. She is not following rules; she is simply doing journalism. If she is a crime reporter, she produces "murder of the day" stories. If she is a court reporter, she writes stories about the most recent trials., and much like cell reproduction, occasionally, she makes a mistake. The word "mistake" may be too strong—I mean by it that she may do something out of the ordinary, unusual, or outside convention. She may, for instance, fail to gather enough facts or gather the wrong facts. Notice that the mistake made is more in the way of "doing something with which other journalists may disagree or that they may not understand." She may not know she has made a mistake until someone calls on her to account for her actions.

The rules of journalism are a natural response to this call to account for behavior. Suppose, for example, someone challenges the facts our journalist has gathered. "These aren't facts," this person may say. "They are nothing more than opinion!" She may respond by saying something like, "The information I have gathered is factual because it has been verified by more than one legitimate source." Here is a rule of journalism: a "fact" is defined as a bit of information that has been confirmed by an authoritative source. Journalism is made sensible by such rules, or put another way, it is recognizable by the repertoire of justifications that journalists have developed to account for the practice.

Most often, a reporter is asked to account for *how* she has reported the news: Has she sought out the right sources? Has she balanced one source with others who might disagree? Has she attributed key facts to appropriate sources? Challenges to this sort of behavior elicit what we have called *regulative* rules: rules about how to do journalism. If challenged on whether an item in her story is a fact, our reporter will respond with a rule about how a reporter typically gathers facts: "I checked for facts in this place and wrote them down in this way." Having to do so is quite common. Journalists are asked all the time by editors, other reporters, and readers to explain their news decisions. Why did you write the lead this way? Why did you put this information first? Why did you use this source?

More rarely, journalists encounter a more basic challenge. A reader may ask, not "Why did you gather these facts" but "Why are you gathering facts at all?" Such challenges invite a reporter to consider not *how to do* journalism, but what journalism, at bottom, *is.* The proper response to such a question, of course, is that journalists gather facts about events, full stop. Here, we see a different type of rule, a *constitutive* rule. Constitutive rules do not tell us how to do something; rather, they define what something is. Journalism *is* an activity in which people gather facts. Whenever we encounter journalists using "is" statements of this kind (news "is" this or that) we know that we dealing with constitutive rules about what counts as journalism.

We might ask how reporters know that journalism is an activity in which people gather facts, and the only good response is "because they say it is." By "they" I mean members of the community in which journalism is a recognized activity. These folks agree that journalists gather, and ought to gather, facts. In this agreement they make it so. Here we see that the rules of journalism, in the end, are nothing more than intersubjective agreements about how things are or ought to be within a community of understanding. Wittgenstein (1958, ¶ 241) calls this kind of agreement a form of life. "So you are saying that human agreement decides what is true and what is false?" he has his interlocutor ask. To which he responds, "It is what human beings *say* that is true and false; and they agree in the language they use. That is not agreement in opinions but in form of life" [italics in original]. Were someone really to ask our reporter why she must gather facts to write the news, her response is likely to end at "Journalism entails fact gathering." If pressed further, she will simply repeat, "This is what journalism is" (which implies "so this is what I do").

Let's stop here for a moment, to ask why a journalist would ever agree to play this game of accounting for her behavior. What's in it for her? This is a question about the relationship between individuals and the social fields they inhabit. It has two answers. One answer is functional: a facility with the rules of the game allows a player to win. Win what? She may win the symbolic (status, prestige) and material (money) forms of capital that accumulate within the field of journalism. The other answer is more purely symbolic. By learning the repertoire of justification within journalism, a journalist becomes recognizable to others and to herself. She *becomes* a journalist. Less tangible than money, or even prestige, the lure and power of identity for inhabitants of social fields.

What has all this to do with the public? Let's continue with our prior example. Suppose that our journalist is challenged about why she is gathering facts, and she responds, "Journalism is a practice in which people gather facts." We may also imagine her going a bit further, to say something like "and journalists gather facts so that readers have correct information." If she made this move, the game continues. "But why should people have correct information?" "So that they can form opinions about the issues discussed in the news." "Why do they need to form opinions?" "So that policymakers know what the public wishes them to do." "And why do policymakers need to know what the public wants?" "Because in a democracy, public policy is, or ought to be, guided by public opinion." Here we come to another constitutive statement, or statement of what is. Democracy *is* a political practice that is responsive to public opinion., and we have arrived at a final crucial point: the constitutive rules of journalism are not the ontological bottom of the practice because journalism is implicated in something larger than itself—the broader constitutive commitments of public life. This is what it means to say that journalism is a public activity. Because it is a public activity, journalism's constitutive rules are entangled with broader social rules about how things stand, or ought to stand, in public life generally. The final appeal to what journalism is, and why it is this and not something else, is not to journalism per se but to the constitutive commitments of the form of public life in which it is embedded.

This realization brings us to two final points. First, the composition of journalism's repertoire of justification is shaped in part by its position in public life. A journalism pulled strongly by the market, for instance, will be different from a journalism that feels the influence of civil society. Knowing this helps us to understand cross-national differences, as well as differences between organizations located in different positions within the field of journalism. Second, the connection between journalism and public life tells us something about the boundaries of the field. These boundaries lie at the limits of recognition, specifically, at the limits of the practices, values, and identities that can be justified, and recognized, as journalism. These limits, of course, end in the constitutive commitments of public life.

Mapping Change

With this refresher, we may now ask what it means to say that journalism is *changing*. The question of change has become more pressing of late, primarily due to the rise of new digital technologies. It is important to recognize that these technologies have not fallen out of the sky. Rather, they have been developed primarily as part of the market, in the form of cell phones and tablets, desktop computers and wireless routers, websites and apps (see Figure 5.2). This isn't wholly true. Government agencies more or less invented the Internet, for instance, and nonprofit foundations—especially the Knight Foundation—have been instrumental in bringing a more technological mindset to journalism. But it is mainly true. People inventing the new tools primarily work for technology *companies*, emphasis here on companies. This will become important to our story when we consider how journalists have responded to the disruption of their field. Here, it is enough to see that the forces of disruption have arrived in journalism from outside the field, and have come primarily from the market.

In the main, new digital technologies have had two effects on the field. First, they have made it possible for anyone to produce news, and to distribute this news at a scale once reserved for media outlets (Benkler, 2006; Shirky, 2008). We now live in an information-saturated world, one in which news outlets compete

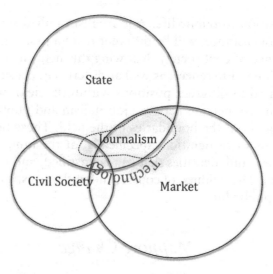

Figure 5.2   A Deflated Field of Journalism

with many others for the scarce attention of audiences. Second, this opening of the communication space has decimated the business model of legacy media. This is most true in the United States, but journalism everywhere has felt the effects of this shift (Levy and Nielsen, 2010). The business model of news depended precisely on attention abundance, that is, on the fact that audiences (and therefore advertisers) had no one else but them as sources of news and information. Regional newspapers in particular have lost their monopoly on the attention of local audiences, and revenues have plummeted as a result. In the United States, advertising revenue in the newspaper industry now stands at a level last seen in the 1950s, a time when the U.S. economy was much smaller (Pew Research Center, 2015). Less revenue has meant fewer journalists. Again, in the United States, roughly 30 percent of daily journalists have lost their jobs in the last ten years alone (Waldman, 2011). Similar economic tremors have been felt in journalism around the world.

To understand what this has meant for journalism, return to the tent metaphor above. If modern journalism inflated amid the pushing and pulling between the state, the market, and the profession, then in contemporary journalism one of these poles—the market—has lost a great deal of strength. In this condition, the tent loses tension, and begins to sag. Essentially, this is what has happened to American journalism. As the force of the market has weakened, there is less for the forces of the state and of the profession to push against. In the event, the field of journalism has lost integrity. Its boundaries have become more permeable, and there are fewer journalists available to patrol those boundaries.

Journalism has felt these effects anywhere it is strongly exposed to the market. In the U.K., for instance, more than 300 local newspapers have closed in the past ten years, and upwards of half of the journalists working for these newspapers have lost their jobs (Turvill, 2015). In other parts of the world, where journalism is not so exposed to the market, the change in journalism has been less dramatic. A recent comparison of journalism in Seattle, Washington, and Toulouse, France illustrates the difference (Powers et al., 2016). In Seattle in recent years, newspaper circulation has declined nearly 40 percent, hundreds of jobs have been lost, and a daily newspaper that had existed for more than one hundred years shuttered its doors. In contrast, in Toulouse during the same period, newspaper circulation has increased and the loss of journalism jobs has been minimal. Online, the differences are just as stark. Seattle has witnessed the emergence of dozens of online news organizations, while in Toulouse only two have appeared. What accounts for the difference? Mostly, it is due to the fact that French journalism is far less exposed to market forces, and subsidized more by the government.

A similar story can be told of the rest of Europe (Nielsen, 2016b). In Scandinavia, for example, mainstream news outlets are losing audiences, but this seems as much to do with a lack of relevance (especially to young people) than to a major technological disruption of the field. Similarly, Scandinavian news organizations are feeling more economic pressure, but nothing like the existential crisis that has afflicted American journalism (Hjarvard and Kammer, 2015). For example, they have not experienced a great contraction of the labor market for reporters. Moreover, traditional media organizations have retained the wherewithal to incorporate new digital media players rather than be challenged by them from the outside.

In places like the U.S., and the U.K., where the economic tremors have been greatest, predictable results have followed: more and different kinds of people and organizations are producing news in the social space once occupied solely by journalists (see Figure 5.2). In most regions of the United States, for instance, dozens and in some cases hundreds of online-only news sites have emerged (Ryfe et al., 2012)., and in the U.K., one census (Ponford, 2015) has counted the emergence of 550 ultra-local news sites. To many observers, this process has meant the nearly complete unraveling of the field (Deuze, 2007; Hermida, 2014; Jarvis, 2009; Shirky, 2008). Journalism, a popular saying goes, has become a "natural act" that anyone can perform.

A great number of new practices have emerged in the wake of this disruption. Among others, they include news as aggregation and curation, citizen and pro/am journalism, journalism as coding, and branded journalism. One way to think of these new practices is that they have increased the number of mistakes taking place in the field. Again, I mean by "mistake" the number of instances in which journalists do something that might be unfamiliar, and even unrecognizable, to others in the field, and therefore, the number of instances in which they might be asked to account for their activities. The question is whether, and the extent to which, any of these mistakes constitute a change in journalism, and, if so, what kind of change this might be.

Before answering these questions, we should remind ourselves that mistakes in the practice of news production have always been more or less common. As we know, they are typically handled by an appeal to the reservoir of shared justifications available in the field. A mistake that cannot be justified is one that typically merits a rebuke. A change, then, in these terms, is distinguished from a mistake by the fact that it generates a new justification. Journalists are always finding new ways to achieve conventional purposes. They are, in other words, always making mistakes. Change happens when a pattern of mistakes multiplies to the extent that it generates a new justification. New justifications create new meanings and new relationships within the field. They change the way things stand between journalists, and between journalists and others. It is the alterations in how things stand between people in the field that constitute change.

Focusing a discussion of change on justifications rather than on actions adheres to our general sense that the rules of journalism hang together as intersubjective agreements about how things stand, or should stand, between us. It does something more. It allows us to see that different kinds or scales of change are possible. As we have learned, justifications tend to be of two types: appeals to regulative rules about how to do something, and appeals to constitutive rules about what something is. These represent different sorts of changes. An example will help us to see the difference.

Consider for a moment the practice of verification in digital environments. The "this, this, and then this" of verification has been long established in journalism. For instance, a reporter who has gathered a significant fact for a news story must, among other things, confirm that fact with multiple authoritative sources; quote sources accurately and in context, and be transparent about where and how the fact was obtained. She must perform all of these actions *before* a story is published. No two journalists may perform these actions in precisely the same way (Shapiro et al., 2013). But every journalist knows these rules, and a violation of them may lead to a request to account for one's behavior: Why didn't you check with more than one source?!

Live television reporting of the kind practiced by CNN began to pull at these traditional verification practices already in the early 1990s. But digital environments—blogs, Facebook, Twitter, and so on—have greatly exacerbated the tension. These are forums where claims circulate freely, mount quickly, and become detached from their original sources instantly (Hermida, 2015). As such, digital environments present an acute problem for the traditional practice of verification: by the time reporters go through their "this, this, and this" process to verify claims made in these arenas, the conversation may have moved on. But if they don't take the time to verify claims before they publish, then they are acting no differently than anyone else in the conversation. That is, they are no longer acting like journalists. Journalists find this a difficult position to be in, yet it is one that they routinely confront in digital environments.

Journalists have had a variety of responses to this situation. One flatly rejects information published via digital media unless it can be verified in the traditional way (Kovach, 2005). Journalists who reject the new practices essentially insist that there is no justification for them. In their view the new practices are not journalism, nor should they be.

Others have embraced the new practices. For instance, some journalists now publish first and verify after (Bruno, 2011). The idea is to publish information when it becomes known, tag it as unverified, and then update as events progress. Another approach is for news organizations to create teams of reporters dedicated to verifying digital information before it is published (Newman, 2009). Still other news organizations outsource verification to third-party organizations like Storyful (Silverman, 2011). Some hold out hope for the invention of new digital tools that can automatically sift through and verify information circulating through social media (Diakopoulous et al., 2012; Schifferes et al., 2014). To the extent that they deviate from the "this, this, this" of traditional verification processes, it is fair to say that these new practices may represent a change in journalism. But of what kind?

If we return to the arena of justifications, we find two answers to this question. One argues for a limited change while another points to a more fundamental change.

The first has journalists adopting the new practices, but justifying them in traditional terms. For instance, after a review of social media policies adopted by seventeen news organizations, the American Society of News Editors (ASNE) published a guide: "10 Best Practices for Social Media: Helpful Guidelines for News Organizations" (Holman, 2011). Its number-one best practice: "Traditional Ethical Rules Still Apply Online." Among other things, this means that journalists should "verify anything on a social networking site before reporting elsewhere." Here, the new practices are made sense of in old terms. It is perfectly fine to crowdsource the process of verification, this guide suggests. But journalists should still verify the information, and verify it before they disseminate it to audiences. This is change of a kind. Certainly, the reporters who adopt the new practices experience them as a change from the past. Yet it is change limited to the level of practice, one that ultimately reconfirms a more basic, constitutive definition of journalism, namely, that it is a practice of verification *before information is published.*

The empirical literature indicates that, so far at least, this is precisely what has happened with most new digital practices. Observations of and interviews with journalists, as well as content analyses of journalism, confirm that most professionals make sense of the new digital tools via longstanding justifications (Boczkowski, 2004; Chung, 2007; Domingo, 2008; Ryfe, 2012; Singer, 2004). Or, as O'Sullivan and Heinonen (2008) conclude, the story of digital journalism is one of "Old Values, New Media."

A second kind of change is more fundamental. Many observers argue that new digital practices are forcing basic, constitutive changes in journalism. Lewis (2012, p. 851), for instance, identifies an "ethic of participation" emergent in forms of journalism like these new verification practices (see also Singer et al., 2011). Robinson refers to the same phenomenon as a new form of "journalism as process," and Hermida (2010) as the rise of "ambient journalism." Such labels—"fluid journalism," "hybrid journalism," and "open-source journalism" have also been suggested—all imply that a significant change is underway.

The evidence for this change comes from examples such as that of Andy Carvin, a former senior strategist for National Public Radio (NPR). Carvin's live-tweeting of the Arab Spring uprising of 2011 is often taken to embody the new ethic of participation scholars glimpse in digital journalism. Carvin famously crowd-sourced tweets about the Arab Spring on his personal Twitter feed, thus creating what Silverman (2011) calls a "living, breathing, real-time verification system" (see also Hermida, 2014). As we know, however, to discern whether his new practices constitute change, it is necessary to focus less on the actions themselves than on justifications for them. Carvin has provided such justifications in response to critics such as Michael Wolff. While admitting that Carvin has invented a "new form of journalism," Wolff (2012) suggests that Carvin is interested less in verifying information than in "propagate[ing] misinformation." Carvin obviously disagrees. But what are his reasons for doing so? His arguments in support of the new practices provide a glimpse into the justifications that lay beneath them.

Many of his arguments appear in a keynote address Carvin (2013) delivered just after the Boston bombing, an event during which a great deal of misinformation was distributed via social media. Carvin begins his account with a rear-guard defense. "Errors," he argues, "have always been part of journalism." In other words, journalists have always struggled to verify information, and sometimes they get it wrong. That was true in the heyday of print journalism and it is true in the era of social media. Then, Carvin admits that social media may have exacerbated the "pressure to keep the public updated as quickly as possible." But, he argues, there is no going back to a time before social media. "We no longer control the flow of information. *We are no longer the media*" (italics in original). The only choice is to go forward. "I think," he states, "we need to get back to a core part of journalism, and rethink what it means to inform the public." No longer should journalists imagine their role to be informing the public. Instead, Carvin suggests that they should see their role as one of "creat[ing] a more informed public." In this use of the conditional voice (what journalists "should" do), Carvin offers a new constitutive image for a "core part of journalism." To him, journalism is, or should be, a practice of creating an informed public.

The notion that journalism should inform the public imagines journalists as information gatherers and news producers: people who gather and verify facts, write stories, and disseminate them to citizens. Creating an informed public demands more. As Carvin notes, it requires journalists to talk to citizens, argue with them, collaborate with them, and challenge them. "If we are going to embrace the notion of creating a more informed public," Carvin concludes, "reporting is no longer enough. We must work harder to engage them, listen to them, teach them, learn from them. We must help them [become] better producers, as well as consumers, of information." Here, we see that Carvin's justification ends in an "is" statement: journalists are (or should be) teachers, listeners, and students. This is the sort of change scholars and others point to when they declare that journalism is being reconsidered, rethought, and so on. It is not only that the practice of digital journalism is different, Carvin insists. It is, he argues, that the new practices change what journalism *is*, and ought to be.

As Carvin's example illustrates, those who argue that journalism is experiencing a fundamental change are not wrong. But they may be premature. Carvin's sense of what journalism should or could be has won few converts in the field. As the ASNE best practices guide demonstrates, even today most news is verified most of the time in the traditional way, and new practices are incorporated into longstanding notions of what journalism is and should be. This is the point at which confusion often sets in. Many observers may glimpse in the new practices new constitutive rules for what journalism is. Just look at what people like Carvin are doing, they insist, and how Carvin justifies what he does! At the same time, few journalists accept the new justifications, and longtime justifications remain in place. So, are the observers right or not? Is journalism undergoing a fundamental change or isn't it?

To help dispel this confusion, we might bring in the element of time. When confronted with contrary evidence, supporters of the idea that journalism is changing often make a temporal appeal. That is, they argue that the new way of thinking has not won the day—yet. It is, they insist, only a matter of *time*. Let's take a moment to reflect on how time is implicated in change.

Time and Change

Generally speaking, change in a social field happens on one of two time scales: incrementally, over a long period of time, or all at once, as in a crisis. An example of incremental change is the "rise of contextual journalism" that Fink and Schudson (2014) detect in American journalism of the past fifty years. Before the 1960s, they argue, "the culture of the press was cooperative, even complaisant" (p. 2). Journalists rarely pressed officials, rarely revealed information officials wished to be kept secret, and published verbatim reports of events provided by officials. Over several decades, these practices began to change. Reporters became more critical of officials. Their reports became more interpretive (Hallin, 1994). They wrote longer stories that included fewer official statements and more of their own voice (Barnhurst and Mutz, 1997). This change happened in the United States first, and in the ensuing decades swept across Europe (Esser and Umbricht, 2014). The result, Fink and Schudson (2014) suggest, has been more "contextual journalism," news oriented less to "documenting the important events of any given day and more about providing context" (p. 7). This change happened so slowly that journalists themselves often fail to perceive it (Barnhurst, 2016).

Change might also happen in crisis. The archetypal example is one we have already discussed: the demise of the American party press system in the late nineteenth century. Through that century, journalists invented many new forms of journalism, from the summary lead to the inverted pyramid style of writing, the interview to objectivity. Over that entire time, however, the party press remained more or less intact, and journalism retained its basic shape (Kaplan, 2002; Ryfe and Kemmelmeier, 2010; Schudson, 1998). It was only in the aftermath of crisis, specifically, the breakdown of the third party system in the late 1890s (Kaplan, 2002), that journalism dramatically changed. That crisis swept aside the old system, opening an opportunity for the new practices to jell together into a new, more modern form of journalism.

When observers argue that journalism is being disrupted, rethought, or reconsidered, they often have in mind that journalism is undergoing a crisis. But think again about what this would entail. The last great shock to American journalism—the transition from the nineteenth-century press to twentieth-century modern journalism—involved not simply a change in journalism but a widespread societal upheaval. In economics the coming of the second industrial revolution; in politics the emergence of mass democracies; in society the rise of professions; and in technology the invention of printing presses capable of mass production. As we know, journalism is entangled in contiguous social fields, especially politics and economics, but also the arts, civil society, and technology. As such, it cannot experience a crisis sufficient to change its basic form absent a wider crisis in these other social fields.

Observing the current scene, there seems to be only one contender for such a crisis, and that is the rise of a networked society (Castells, 1996; van Dijk, 2012). Scholars across the humanities and sciences have detected shifts in society away from centralized, homogeneous, and bureaucratic forms of life toward decentralized, plural, post-bureaucratic forms. Political scientists write of the rise of new networked political organizations (Bimber, 2003; Bimber et al., 2012; Howard, 2005; Karpf, 2012; Kreiss; 2012; Nielsen, 2012). Sociologists detect new networked forms of social relations (Baym, 2010; Boyd, 2014; Rainie and Wellman, 2012). Economists trace the rise of networked economics (Goyal, 2009; Knoke, 2012). Everywhere, digital technology seems to be offering new ways of linking ourselves to others (Brynjolfsson and McAfee, 2014).

Taken together, the social, political, economic, and civic changes wrought by new technologies seem dramatic. Most considered judgments, however, suggest that the various changes represent more of a layering onto the old than a sweeping away. This is especially the case in politics, where political scientists have been careful to point out that networked politics is an addition to rather than a replacement of the old rules. It is even true in the area of social relations, where the effects of technology are being felt unevenly across age, class, and educational attainment. Everything, it turns out, is not changing. This is true of journalism as well. If new digital forms of economics, politics, and so on represent additions rather than upheavals, it is very likely that new journalistic forms represent the same. This would explain the tepid reaction to the new verification strategies proposed by Andy Carvin and others. Conditions on the ground may change, of course, but as of this writing it does not appear that journalism is experiencing a crisis of a kind and scale that might wipe out its basic rules.

Perhaps, however, the new practices represent an incremental change. Of course, only time will tell, but think about the elements that have gone into the growth of contextual journalism. Scholars trace the rise of interpretive journalism in part to dynamics external to the profession, especially a political culture that became more adversarial and promotional. Processes internal to the profession also played a role. Journalists became better educated. They gained greater access to data, especially social science data., and in the face of a more promotional public culture, journalists became more suspicious of public officials, and consequently more aggressive in their questioning. These external and internal factors interacted in such a way that news production slowly changed.

Something like this process may be happening with digital journalism. External to the profession, digital tools have made possible new forms of collaboration. Organizations that take the best advantage of these tools tend to be smaller (to have fewer employees) and flatter (to have fewer hierarchies). They tend to be less formal and more fluid, less rigid and more nimble. As one example, the boundaries between who works for the organization and who does not are more blurred. Full-time employees interact with part-time workers and contract workers and even, in many instances, hobbyists who pitch in merely because they are interested in the subject. These sorts of organizations are popping up across the economy, civil society, and politics. It is no great stretch to imagine that they may also pop up in journalism. As they do, the structural change they embody may eventually induce a cultural change within the field. This change, as many scholars argue, may make the profession more fluid and participatory, a "hybrid" field featuring new combinations of old and new values and practices. As the saying goes, only time will tell. The rise of "contextual journalism" took place over a thirty- or forty-year period. Digital journalism has been around for roughly fifteen years. We may be in the middle of an incremental change in the field.

In the meantime, it is hard not to be impressed with the resilience and durability of longstanding regulative and constitutive rules in the field. Let's end this chapter with a consideration of this question: How is that the rules of journalism have persisted in the face of great disruption?

Persistence

We have likened new practices to "mistakes," in the sense that they deviate from the normal or expected pattern of behavior. Much as cancerous cells may reproduce faster and faster in the body, so more and more "mistakes" seem to be spinning out of digital journalism. It stands to reason that as the number of mistakes multiplies, we should expect journalism to change. Yet, for the time being at least, the basics of traditional journalism remain more or less intact. Just as an example, take a moment to examine the website of any mainstream newspaper in the United States. For illustrative purposes, I have chosen sfgate.com, the website of the *San Francisco Chronicle.* It is May 5, 2015 at 6:00 a.m., Pacific Time. What do we find? We find a navigation strip at the top that replicates sections of the print product (news, sports, business, A&E, food, living, travel, etc.). We find the page populated by conventional news stories. These stories are mostly about time-honored topics such as real estate development, an earthquake, a murder, a mayor's legislative proposal, a lawsuit filed by a local city. Public officials and experts serve as sources for these stories, as they have done for decades., and the stories are written mostly in conventional forms, like the who, what, when, where lede: "In her first budget since being elected on the promise that she would strengthen public safety in Oakland," one such lead begins, "Mayor Libby Shaaf is pushing a plan to boost the city's police force." What do we find, in other words? We find persistence, specifically, the persistence of *reporting news,* by which I mean the set of practices associated with patrolling beats, interacting with officials and experts, applying standards of newsworthiness, and packaging information in story formulas to produce conventional news stories. What explains this persistence?

In answer to this question, let's first recall that the disruption of journalism has come from outside the field, in the form of new, market-oriented technologies. As we discussed in the last chapter, journalism does not contain a very robust market-based normative vocabulary. Among journalists, it is difficult to sustain the argument that news is, or ought to be, commercialized. Instead, journalists tend to frame the market as an antagonist to good journalism, and they have done so almost since the inception of the field. In fact, prior to the emergence of the Internet, journalists had been waging a decades-long war against the commercialization of news (Ryfe, 2012). Initially, then, journalists mostly saw the new digital technologies as yet another example of the encroachment of commercialism in the news—and summarily rejected them. Through the early 2000s, for instance, it was not unusual for newspapers to consign their web team of one or two people to a corner in the newsroom, and to shovel stories online that originally had been produced for the newspaper.

Use of new digital tools in the field, however, and the new practices they engender, has increased inexorably. Their greater prominence has forced journalists to respond. Reporters have done so mostly in ways that reconfirm a traditional understanding of what journalism is and should be, and who journalists are and should be. My own research indicates that three processes seem to be at work (Ryfe, 2012). I call them habits, investments, and imagination. In each case, journalists approach new tools and practices in ways that reconfirm pre-existing ideas about what journalism is and how it should be practiced.

Let me briefly describe each of these processes with reference to one of the many new situations the practice of digital journalism has presented to journalists. When the Internet first emerged in the mid-1990s, newspapers began to put up online editions of their daily content almost as an afterthought. But once the digital editions went up, it became possible for the online platform to scoop the newspaper. That is, it became possible for reporters to post their stories online the night before those stories appeared in the next morning's newspaper. Ostensibly, readers may already have read the online version—for free(!)—hours before the newspaper they paid for arrived on their doorstep. Everyone knew this did not make sense, but no one did much about it. More than a decade later, there still are no routine ways to deal with the problem (O'Donovan, 2014; Swisher, 2014).

Longstanding news practices are ill suited to address this issue. Consider, for example, the practice of publishing daily stories in the newspaper. Many journalistic instincts are geared to this enterprise. Reporters know precisely what a daily story looks like, and they shape reporting to these ends. They collect only as much information as is needed for the daily story. They write only as many inches of copy as their editor tells them is needed. They organize the information on the page with an implicit understanding that someone will be reading *it in a newspaper*. These instincts are confounded in digital journalism. News sites need to be refreshed all day, not once a day, and its freshest content ought to appear at 8 a.m., hours before most government agencies open, much less produce newsworthy information. In digital journalism, reporters can no longer gather information in the morning and spend the afternoon writing it up for the next day's newspaper.

As we have learned, it is precisely in such moments, when old institutions do not seem to capture the possibilities inherent to new situations, that new institutions tend to emerge.

Editors have made halting steps in this direction. One response has been to dissociate the act of reporting from the newspaper. The logic is this: if what reporters do is produce content, why not have reporters produce content indiscriminately? Initially, reporters might post this content on a web page, or perhaps in a content management system. From there, the content could be pulled into the appropriate platform, whether that is a news site, a newspaper, a radio program, a social media platform, or a TV show. Problem solved! Another has been to go "digital first," meaning to ask reporters to post information to the web when they know it, add/delete/revise that information online during the day, tweet out bits of information continuously throughout the day, then follow up with second-day story in the next day's newspaper.

These new practices may seem perfectly reasonable, but think about the questions they raise. How long should a story be? How much information should it include? Who edits the stories and when should this occur? How can a reporter write a second day-story when she has spent all morning posting and tweeting instead of doing additional reporting? Should reporters even write "stories"?

These questions had long faded into the background of newspaper journalism. The fact that they have been raised again in digital journalism is an indication that the new practices are extraordinary. They are mistakes set loose in the field of journalism. Naturally, someone—in this case the editor who initiated the change—has been asked to account for it. Journalists have asked: why should we produce the news in a stream of undifferentiated content? Why should we "post it when we know it"?

News managers have struggled to craft justifications for the new practice. Technologists—that is, the people who have invented the new tools—often speak of the products they create in terms of the language of the market. For instance, Annany and Crawford (2014) report that the news app designers with whom they spoke tended to think of news in terms of *content*, and of audiences in terms of *users*. They imagined their primary duty to be "deliver[ing] the content users want to receive" (p. 7). Translated: they saw their role as giving people what they want. Such language is foreign to journalists, who prefer to think of news as stories they write rather than content they sell, of audiences as citizens they inform rather than users to whom they cater, and of their purpose as providing citizens what they need, not consumers what they want. This distance between technologists and journalists has left news managers with a puzzle. The most natural move would be to justify new digital practices using the logic with which they were invented: they are market-based tools. Doing so, however, would likely alienate the very journalists who are expected to adopt the new tools.

A new repertoire of justification has grown up in this gap. It orbits around a language of innovation and entrepreneurialism. As an example of this language, consider Sarah Hinchliff Pearson's (2009) discussion of four "hard truths" she argues that journalists must face. A graduate of Columbia's graduate school of journalism, in 2009 Pearson was a fellow at Stanford's Center for Internet and Society. After telling her audience "we are all journalists now" (truth #1), "the glory days of mass media are over" (truth #2), and "the new so-called parasites of journalism are good for democracy" (truth #3), she gets to her main point: "We need," she declares in truth #4, "less nostalgia and more innovation." Innovation is required to ensure that serious journalism survives. Here, innovation fills the gap between the market (the need for a new business model of news) and journalistic practice. Pearson does not imagine that journalists should sell news, or adopt more profitable practices; rather, she expects them to innovate.

This appeal to innovation is now widespread in the field. It is circulated by a great number of "future of news thinkers," as Dean Starkman (2011) calls them, who form a coterie of academics, publishers, news editors, and others who travel the globe talking up the value of innovation at future of news conferences. It is disseminated by a stream of consultants, such as Clay Christensen (Benton, 2012) who argue that it is not the news industry that is in decline, but journalists' "way of thinking about the industry that is in decline." Nonprofits such as the Knight Foundation have also taken up the call. They have made, as Lewis (2012,) notes, "a highly publicized effort to shape the nature of news innovation" (p. 309). Even journalism schools have gotten involved. In the past decade alone, dozens have established centers of media innovation and entrepreneurialism. This repertoire of innovation allows news managers to translate the vernacular of the market into the practice of journalism in ways they hope journalists will recognize.

Going digital first is not, they insist, a matter of making money. Rather, it is a demonstration of entrepreneurialism, an example of how journalists are innovating, trying new things to meet their audiences' needs.

As I say, journalists have responded to these justifications in one of three ways, which I have labeled elsewhere (Ryfe, 2012) as habits, investments, and imagination. In the first instance, the new practices disrupt the habits, the "this, then this, then this" of daily news reporting. On these occasions, journalists report that the new practices make them feel "odd," or "weird." No longer doing what journalists conventionally do, they feel less and less like reporters. These feelings sometimes combine with the deep distrust that has brewed in newsrooms. For the last twenty years, journalists have waged a low-intensity war against what they see as the commercialization of news (Kovach and Rosenstiel, 2001; Roberts and Kunkel, 2002). This has happened even as newspapers have tried everything they can think of to reverse a decades-long decline in market penetration in their communities. Lacking trust, and feeling their professional identities threatened, many reporters react to the new practices in moral terms. They say, "This isn't right!" Or, "This is just another ploy to make money," or, "These guys [editors] are idiots!"

Another reaction common in newsrooms is more strategic and calculating. Many reporters view the "post it when you know it" regime as a slight against good journalism. After all, no good journalist would publish information before it has been fully verified. They connect this thought to the fact that the newspaper still brings in more than 90 percent of their organization's revenue. This leads them to believe that "post it when you know it" is not even sensible in terms that editors value. Why should we invest our time and energy in practices that we all know are inferior, which will not enhance our status among reporters, and that have only a questionable relationship to the organization's bottom line? Put another way, why should we innovate ourselves out of a job? Often, their answer is that they shouldn't, and so they don't. This reluctance stems not from a loss of identity but from a rational calculation of professional self-interest.

A final reaction has more to do with imagination than investments. Frustrated with the slow pace of change in their newsrooms, many editors have made dramatic gestures. They have created entire new processes to make the newsroom "digital first." Often, this entails cutting some positions in the newsroom, inventing others, and then firing the staff and inviting them to reapply for the new jobs. We might ask whether launching an initiative by firing everyone in the newsroom is reasonable. Here, I wish to focus on what happens next, because it illuminates a third way in which the rules of journalism persist. When editors create new positions, usually there are few settled understandings of the requirements of the new jobs. What does a web editor do, for instance, or a social media manager?

If reporters understand little about what these new jobs entail, then the sources with whom they interact understand even less. For example, suppose for a moment that you are a member of the local city council. You have learned the ropes of how to inter- act with reporters. When a social media manager approaches, you may be confused. How are you supposed to interact with this person? Can you pitch them stories, and if so where will these stories appear? In what form? Can you trust a social media manager to honor longstanding principles—to honor your request to convey some information "on background," for instance, or "not for attribution"? If a journalist is no longer a reporter, are you no longer a source? And if not, then what role are you supposed to play?

In such questions we see that the institutions of journalism set a context for journalists to interact with other people who inhabit public life. If those institutions are disrupted, it is easy for people to lose a sense of how to interact with one another., and yet *they must interact*. Success for legions of public relations profession- als depends on their ability to manage the news. Journalists need sources to provide them information that can be transformed into news.

The result is that reporters make a gesture at engaging in prac- tices like posting it when you know it, but then field calls from policymakers, public information offices, corporate communica- tion professionals, and others, as they have always done. In these interactions, they *act* like reporters. Sources pitch them stories, use their news sense to ask pertinent questions, make a judgment about the newsworthiness of the story and then set about produc- ing the story in ways they have done for decades. This is done not out of habit, or out of reporters' investments, but out of a lack of imagination. Reporters and others can imagine a social media manager, they just cannot imagine being a social media manager and a journalist at the same time.

Note that in this example many people outside newsrooms (city officials, PR professionals) help to reproduce the conventions of journalism. As a thoroughly public activity, journalism is entan- gled in contiguous social fields such as politics and the economy.

Individuals in these fields have investments in journalism that may cut against efforts to do journalism differently. Journalists, it turns out, cannot change journalism alone. Because it is imbricated with the state, civil society, political society, and the market, many people outside of the field have investments in the practice. Public officials manage public opinion through the news; public relations professionals disseminate strategic messages through the news; businesses advertise products through the news; and even citizens have investments in the kinds of news with which they are familiar. Journalists cannot adopt new practices without implicating longstanding relationships with others.

The field of journalism retains integrity then, even in the face of great disruption, partly out of habit, partly out of journalists' calculations of self-interest, and, increasingly, out of a lack of imagination. This is not to say that nothing has changed in journalism. It very clearly has. Rather, it is to say that journalism's traditions remain more and less intact even as this change occurs. In the end, it is not difficult for journalists to adopt new practices. However, it *is* difficult for them—and for others who have investments in the field—to justify them as journalism. Perhaps this will change incrementally as the number of mistakes multiplies in the field.

Conclusion

The perspective we have adopted implies a very important point about the study of journalism and change. Strange as it may be to say, detecting changes in journalism may require more attention to social fields outside of the practice, to whether and how these fields are changing, and to what this may imply for journalism. I think here of politics and economics especially, which historically have provided journalism with ballast as it has developed a degree of autonomy and stability. When investigating the future of journalism, it is a natural inclination to focus on, well, journalism. An approach that takes journalism's relationship to the public seriously suggests that we should resist this inclination, at least to some extent. The constitutive rules of journalism are rooted in broader constitutive commitments of public life. It is in these commitments that we will find the future of journalism.

6

Moving Forward

The story of journalism told by the recent literature is a powerful one. It accounts for journalism's emergence and diffusion. It explains why journalism shares family resemblances everywhere but is nowhere precisely the same. It links the study of media systems to news organizations to individual journalistic practices, role conceptions, and values. It shows how and why normative ideas about journalism could or should matter. One source of its power lies, I think, in its relational attitude: the way it positions journalistic practices and values, journalists and news organizations, the field of journalism and contiguous social fields, *in relation to* one another. On its portrayal, journalism is a thoroughly public act, caught in the push and pull of crosscutting and opposing forces in public life. It is this relational aspect that makes the concept of the public so vital for understanding the field.

Yet, for all of its accomplishments, the story is incomplete. As a way of moving the conversation forward, I wish to end this book with a discussion of questions yet to be answered. I pay particular attention to two of the story's most obvious gaps. A first has to do with the fact that most comparisons of journalism across societies have been done in Anglo-America and Europe. Research on other regions of the world is increasing (de Burgh, 2003a; Hallin and Mancini, 2012). There is a growing literature, for instance, on Latin American journalism, and on journalism as practiced in the former Communist states of Eastern Europe. But much of it has not been incorporated into the broader conversation we have reviewed in this book. For other regions of the world, such as Africa or the Arab states, there is simply a lack of research. These gaps represent a clear limit for a theory built precisely on comparison.

The second way in which our story is incomplete is, in its own way, just as obvious: most of the major studies in the tradition have focused on one kind of journalism, namely, political journalism. It isn't that other forms of journalism, say, literary or tabloid journalism, have received no attention. In fact, the study of literary journalism is vibrant, and tabloid journalism has received a fair amount of scrutiny as well. Rather, it is that these forms of journalism have been studied mostly in an isolated fashion, not in relation to the broader journalistic field. If the best understanding of journalism places it in relation to other practices and practices, this represents another edge to our understanding of the field. Just as one example, knowing more of literary journalism may help us to understand journalism's relationship to public arenas such as the arts.

As a way of ending this volume, then, we turn our attention toward what we do not yet know about journalism. To frame this discussion, let's begin with a brief recitation of what we do know.

What We Know

As a start, we should remind ourselves what the story of journalism is *not*: it is not the story of news. Formal dissemination of news stretches back to the seventh or eighth century in China, and to the fifteenth century in Europe. But in one form or another, humans likely have always produced and distributed news. It appears to be a basic human instinct. In contrast, the story of journalism is one of a discrete occupational field composed of news organizations and inhabited by professional reporters. This distinction is important. It allows us to define our object of inquiry with some precision. Though anyone may produce news, not everyone is a journalist. Journalism is a relatively cohesive and relatively bounded social field. It has an inside and an outside; it contains its own culture, its own preferred identities and roles, values and practices. It is the story of journalism, and not of the news, that we have told.

About this story we know a number of things. The importance of the state is one. Journalism emerged as an occupational field first in the United States (and just a bit later in England). Why Anglo-America and not elsewhere? The simple answer is that the state first allowed journalism space to develop in these countries. No state is powerful enough to prevent people from producing and distributing news. Indeed, most are not even strong enough to prevent the appearance of journalists. But the state can prevent the formation of journalism as a more or less autonomous social field. This is as true in France as it is in China. Absent an occupational culture, journalists often lead fragile, itinerant lives, or pursue journalism as a side-job to being a politician or a businessman or a writer. Without an occupational field, they possess little power to defend shared values. Nor are they able to protect themselves from the whims of the most powerful members of their society.

Journalism emerged first as an occupational field in Anglo-America because it is here that the state gave it room to grow. This happened as a matter of law, tradition, and history. Compared to elsewhere, the state was relatively weaker in Anglo-America, meaning that political and civil society enjoyed relatively more protection. Moreover, in the United States the First Amendment lent "the press" a degree of formal protection from state interference. Nowhere else did journalists experience such freedom to maneuver in public space, to interact, and eventually to build a shared occupational culture.

Another thing we know is that state action alone is not sufficient to bring the field into being. Other pressures, from the economy (such as industrialization and the commercialization of news) and from civil society (the rise of professions, for example), are also vital to journalism's emergence. It is not any one of these developments that explains journalism's rise but the relation between them. Journalism emerges in friction caused by the push and pull of the state, the economy, civil society, and the budding profession.

We know that journalism emerged in democratic market societies, but we also know that it may emerge within other configurations of public life. It is tempting to assume that the Anglo-American example is universal. Buoyed by this thought, twentieth-century American leaders often sought to export journalism to nondemocratic societies in the hope of stimulating democratic reform. It turns out, however, that these assumptions are untrue. For example, France is a democratic, market-oriented society in which journalism failed to inflate for decades after it appeared in Anglo-America, and China is a nondemocratic society in which journalism lately has grown. These examples show that journalism may find itself enmeshed more in civil or political society and less in the market (as in France), or it may find itself nearly subsumed within the state (as in China), or it may find itself in some different configuration of public life. The particulars of each national context differ, meaning that journalism is not the natural creature of democratic market societies that observers once assumed.

While we are on the topic, we know that the national context in which journalism emerges is crucial. As we discuss more fully below, it is sometimes argued that media are increasingly globalized, meaning that national contexts are less and less important for how media institutions evolve (Couldry and Hepp, 2013). One would do better to examine networks of cosmopolitan cities—say, from Vancouver to Mumbai—than national contexts for understanding the form and meaning of media, and by extension, news (Punathambekar, 2013). At least in the case of journalism, however, the bulk of research argues against this notion (Flew and Waisbord, 2015). Even in the European Union, where some news organizations operate outside of national context, it appears that national public life still strongly shapes journalism.

We also know, however, that journalism shares a family resemblance everywhere it is practiced. Whether in Brazil or Japan, the United Kingdom or China, journalism contains a familiar set of preferred identities, practices, and values. Everywhere, for example, journalists believe their primary purpose is to tell the truth, and that they, in some general sense, represent the people (or the public). How has this happened? Partly, it comes from the efforts of Western journalists to export their model to other parts of the world. In the early twentieth century, British journalists brought the Anglo-American model to the rest of the empire. Later, as part of its Cold War struggle with the Soviet Union, American journalists brought it to other parts of the world. The similarity also comes from the fact that the Anglo-American model came first, and so set a standard by which journalists elsewhere measure themselves. Chinese reporters, for example, wish to be recognized as professional journalists every bit as much as do Scandinavian reporters. This means, among other things, that they adopt traits journalists in the West might recognize as "professional." It also stems from the position in which journalists find themselves in modern industrial societies. Everywhere, journalists are pitched between the state, the market, and civil society. In each nation, the particulars differ, but there is something universal about the sorts of responses available to journalists as they are pushed and pulled by these forces. The result is a broadly similar profession across the globe.

Finally, we know something of the internal mechanics of the field. Over time, the field of journalism has developed distinctive rules and resources: rules in the sense of justifications for privileged practices, norms, values, and identifies, and resources in the sense of symbolic and material capital that accrue around these justifications. Together rules and resources organize more and less permeable boundaries around what it is possible for journalists to do. They do so through processes of recognition and rewards.

Suppose, for instance, a journalist proposes to write a news story based on the position of the stars in the astrological calendar. Other journalists question her use of astrology. Is this really a legitimate source of information, they ask? We have learned that, ultimately, she justifies her actions through appeal to constitutive rules for what journalism is, and what it is for, which as we know are rooted in logics that emanate from the state, the market, and civil and political society. Her ability to pull off these justifications depends on her ability to convince her fellow journalists to accept her arguments, that is, to recognize her actions as a legitimate instance of the practice. The better she is at justifying her actions, the more resources (salary, prestige) she accrues, the more invested she becomes in the field's rules and resources.

Note several things about this process. First, it introduces a degree of contingency to the field of journalism. Virtually any action might be justified as journalism. Second, the ability of any particular journalist to convince others depends on a host of factors: on their powers of persuasion, on their status in the field, and on elements of the context (if she works for a tabloid newspaper she may have more success than if she works for a prominent mainstream daily). But third, particular justifications and kinds of justifications sometimes are institutionalized, meaning that journalists develop routine habits, and habits of mind, which lend a degree of stability to the field. Journalists produce this stability by repeatedly taking the same sorts of actions, and returning to the same justifications for these actions. In fact, they are given great incentives to do this. The more they take recognizably journalistic actions, the more others perceive them as "ideal" journalists, the more status they may obtain in the field. It turns that while any action might be justified as journalism, in practice a more and less visible, stable, and narrow range of actions are routinely counted as legitimate instances of the practice.

Briefly, these are some of the things we know about journalism. Together, they represent a great advance in our understanding. But there is still a great deal we do not know.

What We Do Not Know

The first and most obvious gap in what we know derives from the heavy concentration of the literature on Anglo-American and European examples. In preparation for writing this volume, I conducted a more or less exhaustive review of the literature. I found that there is very little research on some regions of the world. About journalism in Africa, for example, we know very little (but see Hadland, 2012; Rønning, 2005; Shaw, 2009). The same is true of journalism as practiced in the Arab states (but see Mellor, 2007, 2009; Sakr, 2005), and in some parts of Central and South America. Significant research on other regions around the globe has been completed. For instance, I found a large and growing body of work on journalism in Southeast Asia. As exemplified by Chapter Three, China in particular has received great attention. But one finds work on journalism in Thailand, Malaysia, Indonesia, and on Indian and Japanese journalism as well (Clausen, 2004; Massey and Chang, 2002; McCargo, 2002; Pintak and Setiyono, 2011; Rao, 2009; Rao, 2010; Seward, 2005; Steele, 2011). I also discovered a literature on journalism of the former Communist states of Eastern Europe (Jakubowicz and Sükösd, 2008; Kenny and Gross, 2008; Roudakova, 2008; Splichal, 2001; Vartanova, 2012; Voltmer, 2008). And, of course, work on Latin American journalism is longstanding (Albuquerque, 2012; Alves, 2005; Guerrero and Márquez-Ramírez, 2014; Salwen and Garrison, 2013; Waisbord, 2000, 2009).

However, it is apparent that much of this work has not been incorporated into the broader conversation. There are many reasons for this situation. Partly it is due to the fact that some of the best work on regional journalism has not been translated into English. For better or worse, English has become the language in which researchers share their work with an international audience. So when some of the best work on Latin American journalism is published only in Spanish, or on Russian journalism in Russian, it means that the global conversation about journalism is diminished. Another reason has to do with publication venues. Until very recently, there were few journals that focused specifically on journalism studies, and fewer still that attracted an international audience. Regional studies were published in regional journals, and so even if translated into English they failed to attract a global audience. One example is *Ecquid Novi: African Journalism Studies*, a journal that publishes a great deal of interesting work on African journalism. This work is mostly read by scholars of the region, however, and so does not often rise to the attention of a more global audience. Today, journals like *Journalism* and *Journalism Studies* have become hubs for journalistic research conducted around the globe. But this is a recent phenomenon, and it will be some time before the literature loses its Anglo-American and Western European focus. A third reason may have to do with theoretical inclination. Again, until very recently, regional studies were often pitched in terms of concepts or theories rooted in a particular national or regional context. This made it difficult to assess studies across regions via a common vernacular, and to build a broader theory about how the state in, say, Thailand, shaped journalism in ways similar and different to the UK. This too has begun to change. Ryfe and Blach-Ørsten's (2011) special issue of *Journalism Studies* extends institutional concepts to non-European examples. Hallin and Mancini's (2004) edited book does the same for their three-models approach. Other edited books, such as Siapera and Veglis's *The handbook of online journalism* (2012), contain applications of field theory to various national systems of online journalism. These examples demonstrate that the field is becoming more integrated around a common vernacular.

Still, it is fair to say that journalism's relationship to public life across much of the globe remains more and less unexplored. This has consequences for our understanding of the field. Take, for instance, the case of Arab journalism. Many aspects of its story are familiar. In the entirety of its existence, for example, the state has played a strong role in managing the field of journalism in every Arab society (Ayalon, 1995). Since the 1990s, some of those restrictions have been relaxed, and an explosion of commercially oriented news outlets has ensued (Mellor, 2007). As we have seen, similar stories can be told of journalism in China, Brazil, and elsewhere.

This said, much in the story of Arab journalism is unique to its context. Three features in particular stand out.

One is the role of pan-Arab nationalism, which has stretched the journalistic field across a range of regional political institutions. An obvious comparison is journalism in the European Union (EU). Similar to the Arab context, a growing European identity has led to the formation of regional news outlets in Europe. Compared to the Middle East, however, most news organizations in the EU remain strongly shaped by national context. Assisted by a "satellite revolution" in the region, pan-Arab identity has created a more or less coherent regional journalistic field. As Valeriani (2010, p. 28) suggests, journalism has come to occupy a hybrid space in the Middle East, one that facilitates direct and daily "interactions between national and pan-Arab news operators and news discourses."

Another outstanding feature of Arab journalism is the role of global, mostly Western-owned, news organizations in shaping the commercial market for news in Arab states. News organizations such as the BBC, CNN, and News Corps are strongly competitive in Arab media markets. Again, globalization has influenced many national fields of journalism. Indian journalism, for example, is strongly connected to the global news system (Thussu, 2005). Given the importance of the Middle East to the global political economy and the crises that routinely erupt in the region, however, Arab journalists work side-by-side with Western journalists in a distinctive way. As Mellor (2007) argues, this peculiar position turns Arab journalists into a bridge between the global and the local, helping to translate global (often Western) concerns and values into a vernacular understandable by local elites and audiences (and vice versa).

Finally, in our review of Western examples, we have not had occasion to discuss the role of religion in the journalistic field. In a study of Arab journalism it cannot be ignored. Much as with Confucianism in China, Islam has helped to forge a broad cultural epistemology in the Middle East and other Islam-dominant societies. In a review of ethics codes written by journalistic organizations, Hafez (2002) finds that religion makes a difference. Influenced by Islamic teachings, ethics codes in the Middle East provide for stronger protection of privacy when it comes into conflict with the freedom of expression. They are also more likely to favor national and cultural considerations over freedom of speech. This is not universally true. Hafez finds a few more "modern," or Western-oriented, journalistic codes in the Middle East. Overall he argues that Middle Eastern journalists contribute to and borrow from a transnational discourse on journalism ethics. Still, in the Middle East, Hafez concludes, one finds a "lower degree of freedom when it comes to news touching upon interests of the state, the nation, or religion. [These] codes point to very different loyalties" (p. 244). In part, this difference is due to the role that religion plays in the public life of these societies (see also Pintak and Setiyono, 2011; and Steele, 2011, for discussions of Islam and journalism in other "Oriental" societies).

Given the relational quality of journalistic fields, learning more about the Arab field should shed light on others. At the very least, it will help us detail with more precision just how, and how extensively, Arab journalism shares a family resemblance with the profession elsewhere. We might tell a similar story about journalism as practiced across the continent of Africa, or within the former Communist states of Europe. Learning more about journalism in these societies will fill in parts of the journalistic family tree.

Learning more about journalism as practiced outside the West may accomplish something else. Often, when scholars compare journalistic fields, they use the Western example as a basis of comparison. That is, they tend to ask questions that arise from the Western experience, such as whether journalism practiced elsewhere promotes democracy, and if so, to what extent. It is not that such questions are unimportant. Rather, it is that in asking them we may crowd out other, less Western-centered questions. Closer attention to fields of journalism farther removed from the West may help us develop new questions. For instance, learning more about the role of religion in Arab journalism may illuminate the role of religion in Western journalism, a topic that has not received much attention. Knowing more about how Arab journalists bridge the global and the local may encourage others to explore how, for example, American journalists build that bridge for their own audiences. In these ways, more and richer comparisons may illuminate new questions to be asked of all fields of journalism.

A second obvious gap in our knowledge of journalism comes from scholars' over-riding focus on political journalism. As Zelizer (2012) notes, "scholarship on journalism has long privileged a journalistic world that is narrower than that which resides on the ground" (p. 459) Even a cursory review shows that she is right. Many if not most of the seminal studies of journalism—that is, the most widely cited and influential research—have focused on political journalism: think of Tuchman's (1978) ethnography of city hall reporters, or Cook's (1998) study of "governing with the news," or Hallin and Mancini's (2004) "three models of media and politics." This focus is understandable. The historical connection between journalism and democracy is strong, and journalists tend to stress their political role above others. Still, while it may be true that political journalists represent, as Jones (2009) describes it, an "iron core" of the news system (p. 1), one that revolves around the hard news of political life, it is also true that they are far outnumbered by journalists who produce other forms of news. This fact alone implies that we know less about the journalistic field than we might suppose.

As one example, consider the case of American literary journalism. Even as recently as the year 2000, Hartsock could begin his *History of American literary journalism* by noting that the subject had, to date, received little attention. Historians of literature, Hartsock observes, think the form beneath them, and historians of journalism fail to see anything especially journalistic in the writings of Mark Twain, Stephen Crane, and Theodore Dreiser. With a few notable exceptions (Fishkin, 1985; Robertson, 1997; Sims, 1990), the form had simply fallen through the intellectual cracks as not literary enough for English scholars and not journalistic enough for scholars of the news.

Since Hartsock's lament, there has been a noticeable increase of interest in literary journalism (Canada, 2013; Connery, 2011; Underwood, 2013). Among other things, scholars have found that American literature and journalism were conjoined from the start. Until the second half of the nineteenth century, it was not unusual to see literary prose and the news appear side-by-side in newspapers. In fact, many of the most famous American writers of the nineteenth century and early twentieth, from Mark Twain to Walt Whitman, Stephen Crane to Ernest Hemingway, started out as reporters. The two—literature and journalism—were not finally made distinct until the advent of professional journalism in the 1920s. At that time, mainstream newswriting became more formal and generic and lost its novelistic aspirations. As the New Journalism of the 1960s suggests, however, journalism never severed its connection to literature. At their edges, the two fields have always blended and blurred.

This borderland is ripe for further investigation. Yet to date it has not been incorporated well into the broader conceptualization of the journalistic field. Neither Hallin and Mancini's comparative method nor Cook's institutional approach give much consideration to the relation of journalism to art. Bourdieu's field theory is more amenable, and the literary model of French journalism has received some attention (Benson, 2013; Chalaby, 1996). In the broader literature, however, the field of journalism is mostly positioned between the state, the political sphere, and the market (Willig, 2012). Roeh's (1989) observation, now made decades ago, still stands: there is a general "refusal to deal with and judge newswriting for what it is in essence: storytelling" (p. 162).

This is a lost opportunity. Two paths deserving of further exploration immediately come to mind. One has to do with the constitution of the border between journalism and literature. How precisely do literary journalists negotiate their position in the field of journalism? How do they distinguish themselves from writers and novelists? How do they justify their work? Through appeal to which resources? From whence do these resources come? How are literary journalists' privileged identities and practices similar to and different from those of, say, journalists who work for daily newspapers? As we learned in Chapter Five, scholars increasingly have asked such questions of technologists, who straddle the border between the fields of journalism and the market (Carlson and Lewis, 2015). Perhaps a comparison with literary journalism might add clarity to this process.

Another aspect of literary journalism worthy of further study has to do with how journalists negotiate the relation between truth, facts, and objectivity within the field. As we learned in Chapter Four, this subject lies at the heart of any definition of journalism. However, before the turn of the twentieth century, there was little separation between "writing" and journalism, and so there was little effort to distinguish between different modes of apprehending the truth (Connery, 2011; Fishkin, 1985; Robertson, 1997). The intention of most nonfictional writing was to conjure broadly truthful statements about the world (Canada,

2013). Since a poem might reveal these statements as well as a news story, both were published in the newspaper.

Somewhere around the turn of the twentieth century, however, modern journalism made a decisive break. Newspapers stopped publishing literature, and mainstream journalists began to fill their news stories with discrete facts, and to veer away from broader statements of truth. Indeed, they privileged "the facts" even if it meant occluding the broader truth of an event, issue, or situation. For their part, twentieth-century literary journalists recoiled at this rigid adherence to "the facts." Truman Capote's *In cold blood* (1966), for instance, invents dialogue and even entire scenes. They justified this deviance through an appeal to "the truth." As Underwood (2013) describes them, "their impulse to expose and to dramatize the realities of life . . . became the focus of their writing . . ., and it took precedence over concerns . . . that they were violating the standards that journalistic organizations have used to define factual writing" (p. 3). To literary journalists, mainstream reporters had become slaves to the overly rigid news formulas enforced by the commercial news organizations for which they worked. To mainstream reporters, the writings of literary journalists were little more than fiction, and so jeopardized the special relationship between journalists and the public that, after all, was built on the premise that reporters would only publish verifiable information.

These arguments have been waged on the borders of literature and journalism since the fields separated in the early twentieth century. They have special resonance today, when the rise of digital journalism has once again upset settled agreements on these issues (Peters and Broersma, 2013). Perhaps there is fodder in these debates that may be brought to bear on new questions. Is a blogger a journalist (Singer, 2005)? Or can journalists engage in collaborative news reporting with their audiences—and should they (Hermida, 2010; Lasorsa et al., 2012; Ruggiero, 2004)? How do journalists, technologists, and others negotiate what counts as journalism in these circumstances, and how are these negotiations similar to and different from those that have taken place between literary and mainstream journalists?

Tabloid journalism is another example of a form that, while in existence for decades—by some definitions for centuries—has received relatively modest attention. By tabloid we mean infotainment journalism, a kind of reporting that focuses on scandal and sensationalism, entertainment and consumerism. The amount of tabloid journalism produced has grown considerably in recent decades, thus giving rise to the term "tabloidization" (Dahlgren and Sparks, 1992; Kurtz, 1993). This trend has been prompted by pressures on news organizations to reach larger audiences. These pressures exist everywhere (Esser, 1999; Sparks and Tulloch, 2000), though they are likely expressed differently across national contexts.

Mainstream journalists generally reject the tabloidization trend, and indeed, the form itself. Thus, as Deuze (2005) remarks, like literary journalists, "tabloid reporters and editors operate in the margins and along the edges of professional journalism" (p. 861). However, though they are marginal to the field, tabloid reporters nonetheless insist that they are every bit as much journalists as are mainstream reporters (Bird, 1992, pp. 90–106). They point out, for instance, that they rely on the same newsgathering practices as mainstream journalists. They develop a "nose for news," and, when possible, "stick to the facts." In their more defensive moments, they argue that the news they produce is even more relevant and interesting to readers than that found in the daily newspaper. Their efforts to establish and retain status in the field open another window into the internal constitution of the journalistic field. Three aspects of this process seem especially ripe for more exploration.

A first is one also raised by literary journalism: the relation of journalism to the truth. Recall that literary journalists justify the fabrications that sometimes appear in their stories as an effort to ascertain the truth, in this case defined as the overall "truth of a situation." Tabloid journalists take a different tack. As Bird (1992) observes, these journalists argue that a story is accurate "if it faithfully reports what was said or written by sources" (p. 92) For instance, if an "expert" tells them that UFOs exist, and they accurately report these statements, then they can fairly argue that their reporting has been truthful. This strategy of justification, common across the field of journalism, raises a host of questions that go to the heart of journalistic authority (Carlson, 2009; Eason, 1986; Zelizer, 1990). From whence does such authority arise? How does it implicate journalists' relationship to their sources? Who counts as an expert and why? Placed alongside the means of literary journalists, the strategy implies the existence of a "repertoire of truthfulness" available in the field of journalism. An interesting project might be to map these justifications across the field, and across multiple fields of journalism. How many such repertoires exist? Which kinds of journalists typically appeal to what justifications?

A second insight offered by tabloid journalism has to do with the relation of journalism to popular culture, or put another way, to class distinctions within a society. Bourdieu in particular makes great use of the concept of class in his field theory of society (Bourdieu, 1985). On his view, social fields are defined by classes, which he defines as groups of individuals who occupy similar positions within the space of a social field. Such groupings remain latent until individuals within the social space nominate and name them as distinct classes. In this way, social classes are part of the overall political struggle within social fields to name the distinctions that will be resonant in that social space. As many scholars have noted (Gans, 2009; Sparks, 1992), the study of tabloid journalism nearly demands attention to this struggle. Rhoufari's (2000) argument is typical. As a form of popular journalism, tabloids explicitly align themselves with the "people," construed as the lower classes, and so explicitly reject the "elite" press and its audiences. The correspondence between tabloids and popular dispositions shapes the rules and resources available to journalists who operate in this part of the field., and so the struggle of tabloid journalists to gain recognition in the field of journalism mirrors, to some extent, the broader struggle of the lower classes to gain visibility in public life (Benson and Neveu, 2005; örnebring and Jönsson, 2004).

Because the concept of class is so vital to Bourdieu's theory, and less so to others we have discussed, I have left it out of the main storyline of this volume. But, as tabloid journalism illustrates, it can be useful for assessing particular journalistic fields, and spaces within these fields.

A final contribution of tabloid journalism is that it provides an opportunity for us to think through journalism's relationship to a sphere of society we have not discussed: the realm of the private. More than one scholar has noted that tabloid journalism is distinctive in its focus on consumption and celebrity—topics conventionally associated with the private sphere (Biressi and Nunn, 2008). Its narrative mode also tends to be conversational, gossipy, and confessional—all qualities associated more with private language, and especially with women and women's conversational culture (Jones, 1980). And, of course, women have a long history of being consigned to the private sphere. In all of these ways, tabloids connect journalism to the private sphere (Scott and Keates, 2004), and given that journalism is becoming increasingly tabloidized, more investigation of this connection seems appropriate. How, for instance, are values, practices, and identities conventionally associated with the private sphere being incorporated into the field? How are journalists adopting, adapting, and/or rejecting these values and practices? What are the gender implications of tabloidization for journalists? Such questions seem especially pertinent for digital journalists, who operate in a medium that, some scholars argue, has upended the traditional relationship between private and public (Papacharissi, 2010).

This seems like a proper place to end. We could go on to discuss more areas worthy of greater inquiry. For example, we have said little about the globalization of news (Livingstone, 2012). Some scholars have gone so far as to argue that transnational media call for an entirely new model of journalism, one that displaces the nation-state as a central unit of analysis (Appadurai, 1996). But I think we have done enough to show that the study of journalism is far from complete. Advances made in the past few decades have been spotty in places. Answers to old questions have produced new ones that have yet to be fully grasped. However, as the field moves forward, the concept of the public will remain vital. As I hope to have shown, it is a central term for understanding the nature of the field.

As public life goes, so goes the journalism.

References

Abbott, A. (1988). *The system of professions: An essay on the division of expert labor.* Chicago: The University of Chicago Press.

———. (1993). The sociology of work and the professions. *Annual Review of Sociology, 19,* 187–209.

Albert, P. (2004). *La press française.* Paris: La Documentation française.

Albuquerque, de A. (2012). On models and margins: Comparative media models viewed from a Brazilian perspective. In D. Hallin and P. Mancini (eds.), *Comparing media systems beyond the Western world* (pp. 72–95). Cambridge: Cambridge University Press.

Alexander, J. (1981). The mass media in systemic, historical and comparative perspective. In E. Katz and T. Szecsko (eds.), *Mass media and social change* (pp. 17–51). Thousand Oaks, CA: Sage.

Alexander, J., and Colomy, P. (eds.). (1990). *Differentiation theory and social change: Comparative and historical perspectives.* New York: Columbia University Press.

Alexander, J., Breese, E., and Luengo, M. (eds.). (2016). *The crisis of journalism reconsidered: From technology to culture.* Cambridge: Cambridge University Press.

Allan, S. (2003). Mediating citizenship: On-line journalism and the public sphere: New voices. *Development, 46*(1), 30–40.

Alsop, J., and Alsop, S. (1958). *The reporter's trade.* New York: Reynal.

Altheide, D. L. (1976). *Creating reality: How TV news distorts events.* Beverly Hills, CA: Sage.

Alves, R. (2005). From lapdog to watchdog: The role of the press in Latin America's democratization. In H. de Burgh (ed.), *Making journalists: Diverse models, global issues* (pp. 181–202). London: Routledge.

Anderson, B. (1983). *Imagined communities: Reflections on the origin and spread of nationalism.* London: Verso.

Anderson, C. W. (2013). *Rebuilding the news: Metropolitan journalism in the digital age.* Philadelphia: Temple University Press.

References

Anderson, C. W., and Schudson, M. (2008). News production and organizations: Objectivity, truth-seeking, and professionalism in journalism. In K. Wahl-Jorgensen and T. Hanitzsch (eds.), *Handbook of Journalism Studies* (pp. 88–101). New York: Routledge.

Anderson, C. W., Shirky, C., and Bell, E. (2012). *Post-industrial journalism: Adapting to the present: A report.* New York: Columbia Journalism School.

Annany, M., and Crawford, K. (2014). A liminal press: Situating news app designers within a field of networked news production. *Digital Journalism, 3,* 192–208.

Appadurai, A. (1996). *Modernity at large: Cultural dimensions of globalization.* Minneapolis: University of Minnesota Press.

Atherton, I. (1998). The itch grown a disease: Manuscript transmission of news in the seventeenth century. *Prose Studies,* 21(2), 39–65.

Ayalon, A. (1995). *The press in the Arab Middle East: A history.* New York: Oxford University Press.

Bagdikian, B. (1983). *The media monopoly.* Boston: Beacon Press.

Baker, C. E. (1994). *Advertising and a democratic press.* Princeton: Princeton University Press.

———. (2002). *Media, markets & democracy.* Cambridge: Cambridge University Press.

Baker, K. M. (1990). *Inventing the French revolution: Essays on French political culture in the eighteenth century.* New York: Cambridge University Press.

Baldasty, G. E. (1992). *The commercialization of news in the nineteenth century.* Madison: University of Wisconsin Press.

Bandurski, D., and Hala, M. (eds.). (2010). *Investigative journalism in China: Eight cases in Chinese watchdog journalism.* Hong Kong: Hong Kong University Press.

Barnhurst, K. (2016). *Mister Pulitzer and the spider: Modern news from realism to the digital.* Urbana: University of Illinois Press.

Barnhurst, K. G., and Mutz, D. (1997). American journalism and the decline in event-centered reporting. *Journal of Communication, 47,* 27–53.

Barnhurst, K., and Nerone, J. (2001). *The form of news.* New York: Guilford Press.

Baym, N. (2010). *Personalized connections in the digital age.* Cambridge: Polity.

Bell, M. (1998). The truth is our currency. *The Harvard International Journal of Press/Politics,* 3(1), 102–9.

Benkler, Y. (2006). *The wealth of networks: How social networks transform markets and freedom.* New Haven: Yale University Press.

Bennett, W. L. (1983). *News: The politics of illusion.* New York: Longman.

Benson, R. (2002). The political/literary model of French journalism: Change and continuity in immigration news coverage, 1973–1991. *Journal of European Area Studies,* 10(1), 49–70.

References

———. (2005). Mapping field variation: Journalism in France and the United States. In R. Benson and E. Neveu (eds.), *Bourdieu and the journalistic field* (pp. 85–112). Cambridge, UK: Polity.

———. (2006). News media as a 'journalistic field:' What Bourdieu adds to new institutionalism, and vice versa. *Political Communication*, 23, 187–202.

———. (2009). What makes news more multiperspectival: A field analysis. *Poetics*, 37, 402–18.

———. (2010). What makes for a critical press? A case study of French and U.S. immigration news coverage. *The International Journal of Press/Politics*, 15(1), 3–24.

———. (2013). *Shaping immigration news: A French-American comparison.* New York: Cambridge University Press.

Benson, R., and Neveu, E. (eds.). (2005). *Bourdieu and the journalistic field.* Cambridge, UK: Polity.

Benson, R., and A. Saguy. (2005). Constructing social problems in an age of globalization: A French-American comparison. *American Sociological Review*, 70(2), 233–59.

Benson, R., and Hallin, D. (2007). How states, markets and globalization shape the news: The French and US national press, 1965–97. *European Journal of Communication*, 22(1), 27–48.

Benton, J. (2012). Clayton Christensen on the news industry. *NiemanLab*, accessed on October 23, 2015 at: http://www.niemanlab.org/2012/10/clay-christensen-on-the-news-industry-we-didnt-quite-understand-how-quickly-things-fall-off-the-cliff/.

Bimber, B. (2003). *Information and American democracy: Technology in the evolution of power.* Cambridge: Cambridge University Press.

Bimber, B., Flanagin, A., and Stohl, C. (2012). *Collective action in organizations: Interaction and engagement in an era of technological change.* Cambridge: Cambridge University Press.

Bird, E. S. (1992). *For enquiring minds: A cultural study of supermarket tabloids.* Knoxville: University of Tennessee Press.

Biressi, A., and Nunn, H. (2008). Bad citizens: The class politics of lifestyle television. In A. Biressi and H. Nunn (eds.). *Exposing lifestyle television: The big reveal* (pp. 15–24). Farnham, UK: Ashgate.

Blanchard, M. A. (1986). *Exporting the First Amendment: The press-government crusade of 1945–1952.* New York: Longman Publishing.

Bledstein, B. (1976). *The culture of professionalism: The middle class and the development of higher education.* New York: Norton.

Blumler, J., and Cushion, S. (2013). Normative perspectives on journalism studies: Stock-taking and future directions. *Journalism*, 15(3), 259–72.

Boczkowski, P. (2004). *Digitizing the news: innovation in online newspapers.* Cambridge, MA: MIT Press.

Born, G. (2003). Strategy, positioning and projection in digital television:

References

Channel Four and the commercialization of public service broadcasting in the UK. *Media, Culture & Society, 25*(6), 774–99.

Boudana, S. (2010). On the values guiding the French practice of journalism: Interviews with thirteen war correspondents. *Journalism, 11*(3), 293–310.

Bourdieu, P. (1977). *Outline of a theory of practice.* Cambridge: Cambridge University Press.

———. (1980). *The logic of practice.* Stanford: Stanford University Press.

———. (1984). *Distinction: A social critique of the judgment of taste.* Richard Nice (trans.). Cambridge, MA: Harvard University Press.

———. (1985). Social space and the genesis of groups. *Theory and Society 14*(6), pp. 723–44.

———. (1986a). From rules to strategies: An interview with Pierre Bourdieu. *Cultural Anthropology, 1*(1), 110–20.

———. (1986b). The forms of capital. In J. E. Richardson (ed.). *Handbook of theory of research for the sociology of education* (pp. 241–58). Glencoe, IL: Greenwood Press.

———. (1998). *Practical reason: On the theory of action.* Stanford: Stanford University Press.

Bourdieu, P., and Wacquant, L. (1992). *An invitation to reflexive sociology.* Chicago: The University of Chicago Press.

Bowd, K. (2006). Intersections of community and journalism in Singapore and Australia. *Asia Pacific Media Educator, 17,* 56–70.

Boyd, d. (2014). *It's complicated: The social lives of networked teens.* New Haven: Yale University Press.

Breed, W. (1955). Social control in the newsroom: A functional analysis. *Social Forces, 33*(4), 326–35.

Britton, R. S. (1933). *The Chinese periodical press, 1800–1912.* Shanghai: Kelly & Walsh.

Brubaker, R. (1985). Rethinking classical social theory: The sociological vision of Pierre Bourdieu. *Theory and Society, 14*(6), 745–75.

Brüggemann, M., and Schulz-Forberg, H. (2009). Becoming pan-European? Transnational media and the European public sphere. *The International Communication Gazette, 71*(8), 693–712.

Brüggemann, M., Engesser, S., Büchel, F., Humprecht, E., and Castro, L. (2014). Hallin and Mancini revisited: Four empirical types of western media systems. *Journal of Communication, 64,* 1037–65.

Bruno, N. (2011). *Tweet first, verify later? How real-time information is changing the coverage of worldwide crisis events.* Oxford: Reuters Institute for the Study of Journalism, accessed on October 23, 2015 at: http://reutersinstitute. politics.ox.ac.uk/publication/tweet-first-verify-later.

Brynjolfsson, E., and McAfee, A. (2014). *The second machine age: Work, progress, and prosperity in a time of brilliant technologies.* New York: W.W. Norton.

References

Buck-Morss, S. (2000). Hegel and Haiti. *Critical Inquiry, 26*, 821–65.

Burgh, de H. (2003a). Kings without crowns? The re-emergence of investigative journalism in China. *Media, Culture & Society, 25*, 801–20.

———. (2003b). *The Chinese journalist: Mediating information in the world's most populous country*. London: Routledge.

Calhoun, C. (ed.). (1992). *Habermas and the public sphere*. Cambridge, MA: MIT Press.

Calhoun, C., LiPuma, E., and Postone, M. (eds.). (1993). *Bourdieu: Critical Perspectives*. Chicago: University of Chicago Press.

Canada, M. (2013). *Literature and realism: Inspirations, intersections, and inventions from Ben Franklin to Stephen Colbert*. New York: Palgrave Macmillan.

Canel, M. J., and Voltmer, K. (eds.) (2014). *Comparing political communication across time and space: New studies in an emerging field*. New York: Palgrave Macmillan.

Caplow, T. (1954). *The sociology of work*. Minneapolis: University of Minnesota Press.

Capote, T. (1966). *In cold blood*. London: Random House.

Cappella, J., and Jamieson, K. H. (1997). *Spiral of cynicism: The press and the public good*. Oxford: Oxford University Press.

Carey, J. (1987). The press and public discourse. *Center Magazine, 20*, 4–32.

———. (1989). *Communication as culture: Essays on media and sociology*. Boston: Unwin Hyman.

Carlson, M. (2009). Dueling, dancing, or dominating? Journalists and their sources. *Sociology Compass, 3*(4), 526–42.

Carlson, M., and Lewis, S. (eds.) (2015). *Boundaries of journalism: Professionalism, practices and participation*. New York: Routledge.

Carr-Saunders, A. M., and Wilson, P. (1964). *The professions*. New York: Frank Cass.

Carvin, A. (2013). Can social media help us create a more informed public? Accessed on October 23, 2015 at: http://www.andycarvin.com/?p=1773.

Castells, M. (1996). *The rise of the network society*. Oxford: Blackwell.

Censer, J. (1994). *The French press in the age of enlightenment*. London: Routledge.

Censer, J., and Popkin, J. (eds.) (1987). *Press and politics in pre-revolutionary France*. Berkeley: University of California Press.

Chalaby, J. (1996). Journalism as an Anglo-American invention: A comparison of the development of French and Anglo-American journalism, 1830s–1920s. *European Journal of Communication, 11*(3), 303–26.

———. (1997). No ordinary press owners: Press barons as a Weberian ideal type. *Media, Culture & Society, 19*, 621–41.

———. (2004). Scandal and the rise of investigative reporting in France. *American Behavioral Scientist, 47*(9), 1194–207.

Chan, J. M. (2003). Administrative boundaries and media marketization: A

References

comparative analysis of the newspaper, TV and Internet markets in China. In C. C. Lee (ed.). *Chinese media, global contexts* (pp. 159–76). London: Routledge.

Chan, J. M., and Qui, J. L. (2001). China: Media liberalization under authoritarianism. In M. E. Price, B. Rozumilowicz, and S. G. Verhulst (eds.) *Media reform: Democratizing the media, democratizing the state* (pp. 27–46). London: Routledge.

Chan, Y. (2010). The journalistic tradition. In D. Bandurski, and M. Hala (eds.) *Investigative journalism in China: Eight cases in Chinese watchdog journalism.* Hong Kong: Hong Kong University Press.

Charles, A., and Stewart, G. (2011). *The end of journalism.* New York: Peter Lang.

Charon, J. M. (1991) *Le presse en France de 1945 à nous jours.* Paris: Seuil.

Chen, J., and Dickson, B. J. (2010). *Allies of the state: China's private entrepreneurs and democratic change.* Cambridge, MA: Harvard University Press.

Christians, C., Glasser, T. L., McQuail, Nordenstreng, K., and White, R. A. (2009). *Normative theories of the media: Journalism in democratic societies.* Urbana: University of Illinois Press.

Chu, L. L. (1994). Continuity and change in China's media reform. *Journal of Communication, 44*(3), 4–21.

Chung, D. (2007). Profits and perils: Online news producers' perceptions of interactivity and uses of interactive features. *Convergence: the international journal of research into new media technologies, 13*, 43–61.

Clausen, L. (2004). Localing the global: "Domestication" processes in international news production. *Media, Culture & Society, 26*(1), 25–44.

Collins, R. (1993). Public service versus the market ten years on: Reflections on critical theory and the debate on broadcasting policy in the UK. *Screen, 34*(3), 243–59.

Connery, T. B. (2011). *Journalism and realism: Rendering American life.* Evanston, IL: Northwestern University Press.

Cook, T. (1998). *Governing with the news: The news media as a political institution.* Chicago: The University of Chicago Press.

Couldry, N., and Hepp, A. (2013). Conceptualizing mediatization: Contexts, traditions, arguents. *Communication Theory, 23*(3), 191–202.

Curran, J. (1978). The press as an agency of social control: An historical perspective. In G. Boyce, J. Curran, and P. Wingage (eds.) *Newspaper History: From the 17th century to the present day* (pp. 51–75). London: Constable.

———. (1991). Rethinking the media as a public sphere. In P. Dahlgren and C. Sparks (eds.) *Communication and citizenship: Journalism and the public sphere* (pp. 27–57). New York: Routledge.

Curran, J., and Park, M. J. (2000). Beyond globalization theory. In J. Curran, and M. J. Park (eds.) *De-westernizing media studies* (pp. 3–18). London: Routledge.

References

Dahlgren, P., and Sparks, C. (eds.) (1991). *Communication and citizenship: Journalism and the public sphere in the new media age.* New York: Routledge.

Dai, W. (2013). Hybrid journalists—Chinese journalists in an era of reform: Their values and challenges. Reuters Institute Fellowship Paper, Reuters Institute for the Study of Journalism, University of Oxford.

Darnton, R. (1985). *The literary underground of the Old Regime.* Cambridge, MA: Harvard University Press.

Dawes, S. (2014). Broadcasting and the public sphere: Problematising citizens, consumers and neoliberalism. *Media, Culture & Society, 36*(5), 702–19.

Deuze, M. (2005). Popular journalism and professional ideology: Tabloid reporters and editors speak out. *Media, Culture & Society, 27*(6), 861–82.

———. (2007). Convergence culture in the creative industries. *International Journal of Cultural Studies, 10*, 243–63.

Dewey, J. (1922). Review of "Public Opinion." *The New Republic,* May 3, 286–8.

———. (1927). *The public and its problems.* New York: H. Holt and Co.

Di, D. (2011). Between propaganda and commercials: Chinese television today. In S. Shirk (ed.) *Changing media, changing China* (pp. 91–114). New York: Oxford University Press.

Diakopoulous, N., Choudhury, M. D., and Naaman, M. (2012). Finding and assessing social media information sources in the context of journalism. ACM SIGCHI Conference on Human Factors in Computing Systems, Austin, TX.

Dimaggio, P., and Powell, W. (1983). The iron cage revisited: Institutional isomorphism and collective rationality in organizational fields. *American Sociological Review, 48*(2), 147–60.

Domingo, D. (2008). Interactivity in the daily routines of online newsrooms: Dealing with an uncomfortable myth. *Journal of Computer-Mediated Communication, 13*, 670–704.

Dooley, B. (1999). *Experience and doubt in early modern culture.* Baltimore: Johns Hopkins University Press.

Doty, J. S. (2008). *Popularity and publicity in early modern England.* Ph.D. Thesis, University of Iowa.

Downie, L., and Schudson, M. (2010). The reconstruction of American journalism. *Columbia Journalism Review,* accessed on October 23, 2015 at: http://www.cjr.org/reconstruction/the_reconstruction_of_american.php.

Downing, J. (1996). *Internationalizing media theory: Transition, power, culture.* London: Sage.

Durham, M. G. (1998). On the relevance of standpoint epistemology to the practice of journalism: The case for a "strong objectivity." *Communication Theory 8*(2), 117–40.

Durkheim, E. (1893/1933). *The division of labor in society.* New York: The Free Press.

References

Eason, D. (1986). On journalistic authority: The Janet Cooke scandal. *Critical Studies in Mass Communication 3*(4), 429–47.

Edwards, M. (ed.) (2011). *The Oxford handbook of civil society*. Oxford: Oxford University Press.

Ehrenberg, J. (1999). *Civil society: A critical history of an idea*. New York: New York University Press.

Eley, G. (1994). Nations, publics, and political cultures: Placing Habermas in the nineteenth century. In N. B. Dirks, G. Eley, and S. B. Ortner (eds.) *Culture, power, history: A reader in contemporary social theory* (pp. 297–335). Princeton: Princeton University Press.

Eliasoph, N. (2013). *The politics of volunteering*. Cambridge, UK: Polity.

Emery, M., Emery, E., and Roberts, N. L. (1996). *The press and America: An interpretive history of the mass media*. 8th ed. Boston: Allyn and Bacon.

Entman, R. (1989). *Democracy without citizens: Media and the decay of American politics*. Oxford: Oxford University Press.

Epstein, G. A. (2008). Dark journalism: Censorship isn't the only thing wrong with Chinese reporting. The other one is corruption. *Forbes*, July 21, 38–42.

Esser, F. (1999). "Tabloidization" of news: A comparative analysis of Anglo-American and German press journalism. *European Journal of Communication, 14*(3), 291–324.

Esser, F., and Umbricht, A. (2014). The evolution of objective and interpretative journalism in the Western press: Comparing six news systems since the 1960s. *Journalism & Mass Communication Quarterly, 91*, 229–49.

Ettema, J. (2007). Journalism as reason-giving: Deliberative democracy, institutional accountability, and the news media's mission. *Political Communication, 24*(2), 143–60.

Ettema, J., and Glasser, T. (1998). *Custodians of conscience: Investigative journalists and public voice*. New York: Columbia University Press.

Ezrahi, Y. (1990). *The descent of Icarus: Science and the transformation of contemporary democracy*. Cambridge, MA: Harvard University Press.

Ferree, M. M., Gamson, W. A., Gerhards, J., and Rucht, D. (2002). Four models of the public sphere in modern democracies. *Theory & Society, 31*: 289–324.

Figdor, C. (2010). Objectivity in the news: Finding a way forward. *Journal of Mass Media Ethics 25*(1), 19–33.

Fink, K., and Schudson, M. (2014). The rise of contextual journalism, 1950s-2000s. *Journalism, 15*, 1–18.

Fishkin, S. F. (1985). *From fact to fiction: Journalism & imaginative writing in America*. Baltimore: Johns Hopkins University Press.

Flew, T., and Waisbord, S. (2015). The ongoing significance of national media systems in the context of media globalization. *Media, Culture & Society, 37*(4), 620–36.

Forde, S. (2011). *Challenging the news: The journalism of alternative and independent media*. London: Palgrave Macmillan.

References

Fossum, J. E., and Schlesinger, P. (eds.) (2007). *The European Union and the public sphere: A communicative space in the making?* New York: Routledge.

Fraser, N. (1990). Rethinking the public sphere: A contribution to the critique of actually existing democracy. *Social Text,* 1990(25/26), 56–80.

Freedman, D. (2008). *The politics of media policy.* Cambridge, UK: Polity.

Friedland, L., and Nichols, S. (2002). *Measuring civic journalism's progress: A report across a decade of activity.* Washington, D.C.: Pew Center for Civic Journalism.

Friedson, E. (1986). *Professional powers: A study of the institutionalization of formal knowledge.* Chicago: The University of Chicago Press.

Fuller, J. (1996). *News values: Ideas for an information age.* Chicago: University of Chicago Press.

Gang, Q., and Bandurski, D. (2011). China's emerging public sphere: The impact of media commercialization, professionalism, and the Internet in an era of transition. In S. Shirk (ed.), *Changing media, changing China* (pp. 38–76). New York: Oxford University Press.

Gans, H. (1978). *Deciding what's news: A study of CBS Evening News, NBC nightly news, Newsweek, and Time.* New York: Pantheon Books.

———. (2009). Can popularization help the news media? In B. Zelizer (ed.), *Changing faces of journalism: Tabloidization, technology and truthiness* (pp. 17–28). New York: Routledge.

Garcia-Blanco, I., and Cushion, S. (2010). A partial Europe without citizens or EU-level political institutions. *Journalism Studies, 11*(3), 393–411.

Garnham, N. (1983). Public service versus the market. *Screen, 24*(1), 6–27.

Garnham, N. (1993). The mass-media, cultural-identity, and the public sphere in the modern world. *Public Culture, 5*(2), 251–65.

Geertz, C. (1973). Religion as a cultural system. In C. Geertz, *The interpretation of cultures: Selected essays* (pp. 87–125). New York: Basic Books.

Gentz, N. (2007). Useful knowledge and appropriate communication: The field of journalistic production in late nineteenth century China. In R. Wagner (ed.) *Joining the global public: Word, image and city in early Chinese newspapers* (pp. 47–104). Albany: State University of New York Press.

Giddens, A. (1984). *The constitution of society: Outline of a theory of structuration.* Cambridge, UK: Polity.

Glasser, T. (1992). Objectivity and news bias. In E. D. Cohen (ed.) *Philosophical issues in journalism* (pp. 176–83). New York: Oxford University Press.

Gough, H. (1988). *Newspaper press in the French revolution.* London: Routledge.

Goyal, S. (2009). *Connections: An introduction to the economics of networks.* Princeton: Princeton University Press.

Graves, L. (2016). *Deciding what's true: Fact-checking journalism and the new ecology of news.* New York: Columbia University Press.

Greenwald, M., Bernt, J., and Roberts, G. (eds.) (2000). *The big chill:*

Investigative reporting in the current media environment. Ames: Iowa State University Press.

Guerrero, M., and Márquez-Ramírez, M. (2014). *Media systems and communication policies in Latin America*. New York: Palgrave-Macmillan.

Haas, T. (2007). *The pursuit of public journalism: Theory, practice, criticism*. New York: Routledge.

Habermas, J. (1989). *The structural transformation of the public sphere: An inquiry into a category of bourgeois society*. Cambridge, MA: MIT Press.

———. (1996). *Between facts and norms: Contributions to a discourse theory of law and democracy*. Cambridge, MA: MIT Press.

Hadland, A. (2012). Africanizing three models of media and politics. In D. Hallin, and P. Mancini (eds.), *Comparing media systems beyond the western world* (pp. 96–118). Cambridge: Cambridge University Press.

Hafez, K. (2002). Journalism ethics revisited: A comparison of ethics codes in Europe, North Africa, the Middle East, and Muslim Asia. *Political Communication, 19*, 225–50.

Halasz, A. (1997). *The marketplace of print: Pamphlets and the public sphere in early modern England*. Cambridge: Cambridge University Press.

Haldén, P. (2011). *Stability without statehood: Lessons from Europe's history before the sovereign state*. New York: Palgrave Macmillan.

Hall, J., and Ikenberry, J. (1989). *The state*. London: Open University Press.

Hallin, D. (1994). *We keep America on top of the world: Television journalism and the public sphere*. New York: Routledge.

Hallin, D., and Mancini, P. (2004). *Comparing media systems: Three models of media and politics*. New York: Cambridge University Press.

———. (2012). Comparing media systems: A response to critics. In F. Esser and T. Hanitzsch, eds., *The handbook of comparative communication research* (pp. 207–20). New York: Routledge.

Hampton, M. (2004). *Visions of the press in Britain, 1850–1950*. Urbana: University of Illinois Press.

———. (2008). The "objectivity" ideal and its limitations in 20th-century British journalism. *Journalism Studies* 9(4), pp. 477–93.

Hardt, H., and Brennen, B. (1995). *Newsworkers: Toward a history of the rank and file*. Minneapolis: University of Minnesota Press.

Harrison, J., and Woods, L. M. (2001). Defining European public service broadcasting. *European Journal of Communication* 16(4), pp. 477–504.

Hartsock, J. (2000). *A history of American literary journalism: The emergence of a modern narrative form*. Amherst: University of Massachusetts Press.

Hassid, J. (2008). China's contentious journalists: Reconceptualizing the media. *Problems in Post-Communism* July/August, pp. 52–61.

Hatch, N. (ed.) (1988). *The professions in American history*. South Bend, IN: University of Notre Dame Press.

Hayashi, K. (2011). Questioning journalism ethics in the global age: How

Japanese media report and support immigrant law revision. In R. Fortner and P. M. Fackler (eds.) *The handbook of global communication and media ethics* (pp. 534–53). Oxford: Wiley-Blackwell.

Hermida, A. (2010). Twittering the news: The rise of ambient journalism. *Journalism Practice, 4*, 297–308.

———. (2014). *Tell everyone: Why we share and why it matters*. New York: Random House.

———. (2015). Nothing but the truth: Redrafting the journalistic boundary of verification. In M. Carlson and S. Lewis (eds.) *Boundaries of journalism: Professionalism, practices and participation* (pp. 37–50). New York: Routledge.

Hesmondhalgh, D., and Toynbee, J. (eds.) (2008). *The media and social theory*. New York: Routledge.

Hirschman, A. (1977). *The passions and the interests: Political arguments for capitalism before its triumph*. Princeton: Princeton University Press.

Hjarvard, S., and Kammer, A. (2015). Online news: Between private enterprise and public subsidy. *Media, Culture & Society, 37*, 115–23.

Holman, J. (2011). 10 best practices for social media: Helpful guidelines for news organizations. Columbia, MO: American Society of News Editors, accessed on October 23, 2015 at: http://asne.org/Files/pdf/10_Best_Practices_for_Social_Media.pdf.

Hong, J. (1998). *The internationalization of television in China: The evolution of ideology, society, and media since the reform*. London: Praeger.

Howard, P. N. (2005). *New media campaigns and the managed citizen*. Cambridge: Cambridge University Press.

Høyer, S. (2005). The Anglo-American background. In S. Høyer and H. Pöttker (eds.) *Diffusion of the news paradigm, 1850–1900* (pp. 9–19). Gothenborg: Nordicom.

Høyer, S., and Pöttker H. (eds.) (2005). *Diffusion of the news paradigm, 1850–1900*. Gothenborg: Nordicom.

Hu, Z. (2003). The post-WTO restructuring of the Chinese media industries and the consequences of capitalization. *Javnost, 10*(4), 19–36.

Huang, C. (2004). China's state-run tabloids: The rise of "City Newspapers." *Gazette, 63*(5), 435–50.

Iyengar, S. (1994). *Is anyone responsible? How television frames political issues*. Chicago: University of Chicago Press.

Iyengar, S., and Kinder, D. (1989). *News that matters: Television and American opinion*. Chicago: University of Chicago Press.

Jacobs, R., and Townsley, E. (2011). *The space of opinion: Media intellectuals and the public sphere*. New York: Oxford University Press.

Jakubowicz, K., and Sükösd, M. (eds.) (2008). *Finding the right place on the map: Central and Eastern European media change in a global perspective*. Chicago: University of Chicago Press.

References

Janowitz, M. (1957). *Community ties in an urban setting*. Glencoe, IL: Free Press.

Jarvis, J. (2009). *What would Google do? Reverse engineering the fastest growing company in the history of the world*. New York: Harper Collins.

Jeffres, L. W., Dobos, J., and Lee, J. W. (1988). Media use and community ties. *Journalism & Mass Communication Quarterly, 65*(3), 575–81.

Jones, A. (2009). *Losing the news: The future of news that feeds democracy*. New York: Oxford University Press.

Jones, D. (1980). Gossip: Notes on women's oral culture. *Women's Studies International Quarterly, 3*(2–3), 193–8.

Judge, J. (1996). *Print and politics: "Shibao" and the culture of reform in late Qing China*. Stanford: Stanford University Press.

Kaniss, P. (1991). *Making local news*. Chicago: University of Chicago Press.

Kaplan, R. L. (2002). *Politics and the American press: The rise of objectivity, 1865–1920*. Cambridge: Cambridge University Press.

Karpf, D. (2012). *The MoveOn effect: The unexpected transformation of American political advocacy*. Oxford: Oxford University Press.

Keane, J. (1991). *The media and democracy*. Cambridge, UK: Polity.

Kenny, T., and Gross, P. (2008). Journalism in Central Asia: A victim of politics, economics, and widespread self-censorship. *The International Journal of Press/Politics, 13*(4), 515–25.

Knoke, D. (2012). *Economic networks*. Cambridge: Polity.

Koopman, R., and Statham, P. (eds.) (2010). *The making of a European public sphere: Media discourse and political contention*. Cambridge: Cambridge University Press.

Kovach, B. (2005). Toward a new journalism with verification. Speech given before the Society of Professional Journalists, accessed on October 23, 2015 at http://niemanreports.org/articles/toward-a-new-journalism-with-verification/.

Kovach, B., and Rosenstiel, T. (2001). *The elements of journalism: What newspeople should know and the public should expect*. New York: Crown Publishers.

Kreiss, D. (2012). *Taking our country back: The crafting of networked politics from Howard Dean to Barack Obama*. Oxford: Oxford University Press.

Kuhn, R. (1995). *The media in France*. New York: Routledge.

Kurtz, H. (1993). *Media circus: The trouble with America's newspapers*. New York: Three Rivers Press.

Lamont, M., and Thévenot, L. (eds.) (2000). *Rethinking comparative cultural sociology: Repertoires of evaluation in France and the United States*. New York: Cambridge University Press.

Larson, M. S. (1977). *The rise of professionalism: A sociological analysis*. Berkeley: University of California Press.

Lasorsa, D. L., Lewis, S., and Holton, A. E. (2012). Normalizing Twitter: Journalism practice in an emerging communication space. *Journalism Studies, 13*(1), 19–36.

References

Lauterer, J. (2006). *Community journalism: Relentlessly local*. 3rd ed. Durham, NC: University of North Carolina Press.

Lebaron, F. (2003). Pierre Bourdieu: Economic models against economism. *Theory and Society, 32*, 551–65.

Lee, C. C. (ed.) (2015). *The "Internationalizing" of International Communication*. Ann Arbor: University of Michigan Press.

———. (1990). *Voices of China: The interplay of politics and journalism*. London: Guilford.

———. (2000). Servants of the state or the market: Media and journalists in China. In J. Tunstall (ed.) *Media occupations and professions: A reader* (pp. 240–52). Oxford: Oxford University Press.

———, ed. (1994). *China's media, media's China*. Boulder, CO: Westview.

Lee, C. C., He, Z., and Huang, Y. (2006). Chinese Party Publicity Inc. conglomerated: The case of the Shenzhen Press Group. *Media, Culture & Society, 28*(4), 581–602.

Lee, P. (1994). Mass communication and national development in China: Media roles reconsidered. *Journal of Communication, 44*(3), 22–37.

Lerner, D. (1958). *The passing of traditional society: Modernizing the Middle East*. Glencoe, IL: Free Press.

Levy, D., and Nielsen, R. (eds.) (2010). *The changing business of journalism and its implications for democracy*. Oxford: Reuters Institute for the Study of Journalism.

Levy, L. (1985). *Emergence of a free press*. New York: Oxford University Press.

Lewis, S. (2012). The tension between professional control and open participation. *Information, Communication & Society, 15*, 836–66.

Li, R. (2013). Media corruption: A Chinese characteristic. *Journal of Business Ethics, 116*, 297–310.

Liebman, B. L. (2005). Watchdog or demagogue? The media in the Chinese legal system. *Columbia Law Review, 105*(1), 1–157.

Lin, F. (2012). Information differentiation, commercialization, and legal reform: The rise of a three-dimensional state-media regime in China. *Journalism Studies, 13*(3), 418–32.

Lin, Y. (1814/1968). *A history of the press and public opinion in China*. New York: Greenwood Publishers.

Lippmann, W. (1922). *Public opinion*. New York: Harcourt, Brace.

———. (1925). *The phantom public*. New York: Harcourt, Brace.

Liu, A. (1971). *Communications and national integration in communist China*. Berkeley: University of California Press.

Liu, Z. (2012). *Journalism culture in Kunming: Market competition, political constraint and new technology in a Chinese metropolis*. Ph.D. diss. University of Iowa.

Livingstone, S. (2012). Challenges to comparative research in a globalizing media

References

landscape. In F. Esser and T. Hanitzsch (eds.) *Handbook of Comparative Communication Research* (pp. 415–29). New York: Routledge.

Lorentzen, P. (2013). China's strategic censorship. *American Journal of Political Science, 58*(2), 402–14.

Lowrey, W., Brozana, A., and Mackay, J. B. (2008). Toward a measure of community journalism. *Mass Communication and Society, 11*(3), 275–99.

Luhmann, N. (1982). *The differentiation of society.* New York: Columbia University Press.

Lunt, P., and Livingstone, S. (2013). Media studies' fascination with the concept of the public sphere. *Media, Culture & Society, 35*(1), 87–96.

MacKinnon, S. R. (1997). Toward a history of the Chinese press in the republican period. *Modern China, 23*(1), 3–32.

Mancini, P. (2005). Is there a European model of journalism? In H. de Burgh (ed.) *Making journalists* (pp. 77–93). New York: Routledge.

Maras, S. (2013). *Objectivity in Journalism.* Cambridge, UK: Polity.

Maras, S., and Nip, J. (2015). The traveling objectivity norm. *Journalism Studies, 16*(3), 326–42.

March, J., and Olsen, J. (1989). *Rediscovering institutions.* New York: Free Press.

Martin, J. L. (2003). What is field theory? *American Journal of Sociology, 109*(1), 1–49.

Marzolf, M. (1984). American "new journalism" takes root in Europe at end of 19th century. *Journalism Quarterly, 61*, 529–35, 691.

Maslog, C. C. (1985). *Five successful Asian community newspapers.* Singapore: Asian Mass Communication Research and Information Center.

———. (1989). *The dragon slayers of the countryside.* Manila, Philippines: PPI.

Massey, B. L., and Chang, L. A. (2002). Locating Asian values in Asian journalism: A content analysis of web newspapers. *Journal of Communication, 52*(4), 987–1003.

Matheson D. (2000). The birth of news discourse: Changes in news language in British newspapers, 1880–1930. *Media, Culture and Society, 22*, 557–73.

McCargo, D. (2002). Political journalists and their sources in Thailand. In R. Kuhn and E. Neveu (eds.) *Political journalism: New challenges, new practices* (pp. 92–107). London: Routledge.

McChesney, R., and Picard, V. (eds.) (2011). *Will the last journalist turn out the lights?* New York: New Press.

McCormick, B. L., and Liu, Q. (2009). Globalization and the Chinese media: Technologies, content, commerce and the prospects for the public sphere. In C. C. Lee (ed.) *Chinese media, global contexts* (pp. 136–55). London: Routledge.

McGerr, M. E. (1986). *The decline of popular politics: The American North, 1865–1928.* New York: Oxford University Press.

McMane, A. A. (1993). Ethical standards in French and U.S. newspaper journalism. *Journal of mass media ethics, 8*(4), 207–18.

References

McManus, J. (1994). *Market-driven journalism: Let the citizen beware.* Thousand Oaks, CA: Sage.

McNair, B. (2000). *Journalism and democracy: An evaluation of the political public sphere.* New York: Routledge.

Mellor, N. (2007). *Arab journalism: Problems and prospects.* Edinburgh: Edinburgh University Press.

———. (2009). Strategies for autonomy: Arab journalists reflecting on their roles. *Journalism Studies, 10*(3), 307–21.

Mersey, R. (2010). Reevaluating Stamm's theory of newspapers and communities in a new media environment: Toward a new theory based on identity and interdependence. *Northwestern University Law Review, 104*(2), 517–35.

Merton, R. (1950) Patterns of influence: A study of interpersonal influence and of communications behavior in a local community. In P. Lazarsfeld and F. N. Stanton (eds.) *Communications Research 1948–1949* (pp. 180–219). New York: Harper.

Mey, H. (1972). *Field theory: A study of its applications in the social sciences.* New York: St. Martin's Press.

Mill, J. S. (1859/1978). *On liberty.* E. Rapaport (ed.) Indianapolis, IN: Hackett Publishing Co.

Milton, J. (2014). *Aeropagitica and other writings.* W. Pool (ed.) London: Penguin Books.

Mindich, D. (1998). *Just the facts: How objectivity came to define American journalism.* New York: New York University Press.

Mittler, B. (2004). *A newspaper for China? Power, identity, and change in Shanghai's news media, 1872–1912.* Cambridge, MA: Harvard University Press.

Mohr, J. (2000). Structures, institutions, and cultural analysis. *Poetics, 27*, 57–68.

Moore, R. C., and Gillis, T. L. (2005). Transforming communities: Community journalism in Africa. *Transformations 10,* accessed on September 9, 2015 at: http://www.transformationsjournal.org/journal/issue_10/editorial.shtml.

Moy, P., and Gastil, J. (2006). Predicting deliberative conversation: The impact of discussion networks, media use, and political cognitions. *Political Communication, 23*(4), 443–60.

Muñoz-Torres, J. R. (2012). Truth and objectivity in journalism. *Journalism Studies, 13*(4), 566–82.

Murray, W. J. (1991). Journalism as a career choice in 1789. In H. Chisick (ed.) *The press in the French revolution* (pp. 161–88). Oxford: Oxford University Press.

Nathan, A. J. (1985). *Chinese democracy.* New York: Alfred A. Knopf.

Negt, A., and Kluge, A. (1993). *Public sphere and experience: Analysis of the bourgeois and proletarian public sphere.* New York: Verso Books.

Nerone, J. (1995). *Last rights: Revising "Four Theories of the Press."* Urbana: University of Illinois Press.

Neveu, E. (2009). *Sociologie du journalisme.* Paris: La Découverte.

References

Newman, N. (2009). *The rise of social media and its impact on mainstream journalism*. Oxford: Reuters Institute for the Study of Journalism.

Nielsen, R. (2016a). The many crises of Western journalism: A comparative analysis of economic, professional, and symbolic crises. In J. Alexander, E. Breese, and M. Luengo (eds.) *The crisis of journalism reconsidered: From technology to culture*. Cambridge: Cambridge University Press.

Nielsen, R. (ed.) (2016b). *Local journalism: The decline of newspapers and the rise of digital media*. Oxford: Reuters Institute for the Study of Journalism.

Nielsen, R. K. (2012). *Ground wars: Personalized communication in political campaigns*. Princeton: Princeton University Press.

Nieman Reports (2012). *Be the Disruptor*. October 16, 2012, accessed on October 23, 2015 at: http://niemanreports.org/articles/category/cover-story-be-the-disruptor/.

Nip, J. Y. M. (2006). Exploring the second phase of public journalism. *Journalism Studies, 7*(2), 212–36.

Nitoiu, C. (2013). The European public sphere: Myth, reality or aspiration? *Political Studies Review, 11*, 26–38.

Nord, D. P. (2001). *Communities of journalism: A history of American newspapers and their readers*. Urbana: University of Illinois Press.

Nosco, P. (2002). Confucian perspectives on civil society and government. In N. L. Rosenblum and R. C. Post (eds.) *Civil society and government* (pp. 334–59). Princeton: Princeton University Press.

O'Donovan, C. (2014). N+1: learning that print and digital can peacefully coexist. *Nieman Lab*, accessed on August 23, 2015 at: http://www.niemanlab.org/2014/09/n1–learning-that-print-and-digital-can-peacefully-coexist/.

O'Sullivan, J., and Heinonen, A. (2008). Old values, new media: Journalism role perceptions in a changing world. *Journalism Practice, 2*, 357–71.

Olausson, U. (2010). Towards a European identity? The news media and the case of climate change. *European Journal of Communication, 25*(2), 138–52.

Örnebring, H. (2007). A necessary profession for the modern age? Nineteenth century news, journalism and the publich shere. In R. Butsch (ed.) *Media and public spheres* (pp. 71–82). Basingstoke: Palgrave.

Örnebring, H., and Jönsson, A. M. (2004). Tabloid journalism and the public sphere: A historical perspective on tabloid journalism. *Journalism Studies, 5*(3), 293–5.

Ortega, F., and Humanes, M. L. (2000). *Algo mas que periodistas: Sociología de una profesión*. Barcelona: Editorial Ariel.

Overholser, G. (2006). *On behalf of journalism: A manifesto for change*, accessed September 9 2015 at: http://www.annenbergpublicpolicycenter.org/Overholser/20061011_JournStudy.pdf.

Page, B. (1996). *Who deliberates? Mass media and deliberative democracy*. Chicago: University of Chicago Press.

Pan, Z. (2000). Improvising reform activities: The changing reality of journalistic

References

practice in China. In C. C. Lee (ed.) *Power, money, and media: Communication patterns and bureaucratic control in cultural China*. Evanston, IL: Northwestern University Press.

——. (2000). Spatial configuration in institutional change: A case of China's journalism reforms. *Journalism, 1*(3), 253–81.

Pan, Z., and Lu, Y. (2009). Localizing professionalism: Discursive practices in China's media reforms. In C. C. Lee (ed.) *Chinese media, global contexts* (pp. 215–34). London: Routledge.

Papacharissi, Z. (2010). *A private sphere: Democracy in a digital age*. London: Polity.

Park, R. (1922). *The immigrant press and its control*. New York: Harper and Brothers.

Parsons, T. (1966). *Societies: Evolutionary and comparative perspectives*. Englewood Cliffs, NJ: Prentice-Hall.

Patterson, T. (1992). *Out of order*. New York: Vintage Books.

Peacey, J. (2013). *Print and public politics in the English revolution*. Cambridge: Cambridge University Press.

Pearson, S. H. (2009). Hard truth: Traditional journalism must innovate to survive in a changing information climate. *First Amendment Coalition*, accessed on October 23, 2015 at: http://firstamendmentcoalition.org/2009/09/hard-truth-traditional-journalism-must-innovate-to-survive-in-changing-information-climate/.

Peters, C., and Broersma, M. (2013). *Rethinking journalism: Trust and participation in a transformed media landscape*. London: Routledge.

Pew Research Center. (2015). The state of the media 2015, accessed on October 23, 2015 at: http://www.journalism.org/2015/04/29/state-of-the-news-media-2015/.

Pierson, P. (2000). Increasing returns, path dependence, and the study of politics. *The American Political Science Review, 94*(2), 251–67.

Pintak, L., and Setiyono, B. (2011). The mission of Indonesian journalism: Balancing democracy, development, and Islamic values. *The International Journal of Press/Politics, 16*(2), 185–209.

Polumbaum, J. (1990). The tribulations of China's journalists after a decade of reform. In C. C. Lee (ed.) *Voices of China: The interplay of politics and journalism* (pp. 33–68). New York: Guilford.

Polumbaum, J. (2008). *China ink: The changing face of Chinese journalism*. Boulder, CO: Rowman and Littlefield.

Ponford, D. (2015). New research maps 550 independent "ultralocal" news websites in the UK. *Press Gazette*, accessed on October 23, 2015 at: http://www.pressgazette.co.uk/new-research-maps-550–independent-ultralocal-news-websites-uk.

Popkin, J. (1990). *Revolutionary news: The press in France, 1789–1799*. Durham, NC: Duke University Press.

References

Pöttker, H. (2005). The news pyramid and its origin from the American journalism in the 19th century: A professional approach and an empirical inquiry. In S. Høyer and H. Pöttker (eds.) *Diffusion of the news paradigm, 1850–1900* (pp. 51–64). Gothenborg: Nordicom.

Powers, M., Zambrano, S. V., and Baisnée, O. (2016). The news crisis compared: The impact of the journalism crisis on local news ecosystems in Toulouse, France and Seattle, USA. In R. Nielsen (ed.) *The uncertain future of local journalism: The decline of newspapers and the rise of digital media* (pp. 21–34). Oxford: Reuters Institute for the Study of Journalism.

Preston, P. (2009). An elusive trans-national public sphere? *Journalism Studies, 10*(1), 114–29.

Punathambekar, A. (2013). *From Bombay to Bollywood: The making of a global media industry*. New York: New York University Press.

Putnam, R. (1995). Bowling alone: America's declining social capital. *Journal of Democracy, 6*(1), 65–78.

———. (2000). *Bowling alone: The collapse and revival of American community*. New York: Simon and Schuster.

Rainie, L., and Wellman, B. (2012). *Networked: The new social operating system*. Cambridge, MA: MIT Press.

Rao, S. (2009). Glocalization of Indian journalism. *Journalism Studies, 10*(4), 474–88.

Rao, U. (2010). *News as culture: Journalistic practices and the remaking of Indian leadership traditions*. New York: Berghahn Books.

Reader, B., and Hatcher, J. A. (eds.) (2012). *Foundations of community journalism*. Los Angeles: Sage.

Repnikova, M. (2014). Investigative journalists' coping tactics in a restrictive media environment. In M. Svensson, E. Saether, and Z. Zhang (eds.) *Chinese investigative journalists' dreams: Autonomy, agency, and voice* (pp. 113–32). Lanham, MD: Lexington Books.

Rhoufari, M. (2000). Talking about the tabloids. In C. Sparks and J. Tulloch (eds.) *Tabloid tales: Global debates over media standards* (pp. 163–76). Lanham, MD: Rowman and Littlefield.

Richards, I. (2012). Beyond city limits: Regional journalism and social capital. *Journalism, 14*(5), 627–42.

Rieffel, R. (1984). *L'Elite des journalistes*. Paris: Presses Universitaires du France.

Risse, T. (2010). *A community of Europeans? Transnational identities and public spheres*. Ithaca, NY: Cornell University Press.

Roberts, G., and Kunkel, T. (2002). *Breach of faith: A crisis of coverage in the age of corporate newsgathering*. Fayetteville: University of Arkansas Press.

Robertson, M. (1997). *Stephen Crane, journalism, and the making of modern American literature*. New York: Columbia University Press.

Roche, D. (1989). Censorship and the publishing industry. In R. Darnton and

References

D. Roche (eds.) *Revolution in print: The press in France,* 1775–1800 (pp. 3–26). Berkeley: University of California Press.

Roeh, I. (1989). Journalism as storytelling: Coverage as narrative. *The American Behavioral Scientist, 33*(2), 162–8.

Rønning, H. (2005). African journalism and the struggle for democratic media. In H. de Burgh (ed.) *Making journalists: Diverse models, global issues* (pp. 157–80). London: Routledge.

Roudakova, N. (2008). Media—political clientelism: Lessons from anthropology. *Media, Culture & Society, 30*(1), 41–59.

Ruggiero, T. E. (2004). Paradigm repair and changing journalistic perceptions of the Internet as an objective news source. *Convergence, 10*(4), 92–106.

Ryan, M. (1990). *Women in public: Between banners and ballots, 1825–1880.* Baltimore: Johns Hopkins University Press.

Ryfe, D. (2006). News, culture and public life: A study of nineteenth century journalism. *Journalism Studies, 7*(1), 60–77.

———. (2012). *Can journalism survive? An inside look in American newsrooms.* Cambridge, UK: Polity.

Ryfe, D., and Blach-Ørsten, M. (2011). Introduction. *Journalism Studies, 12*(1), 3–9.

Ryfe, D., and Kemmelmeier, M. (2010). Quoting practices, path dependency and the birth of modern journalism. *Journalism Studies, 12,* 10–26.

Ryfe, D., Mensing, D., Ceker, H., and Gunes, M. (2012). Popularity is not the same thing as influence: A study of the Bay Area news system. *International Symposium on Online Journalism, 2,* 144–61.

Ryle, G. 1949. *The concept of mind.* London: Hutchinson.

Sakr, N. (2005). The changing dynamics of Arab journalism. In H. de Burgh (ed.) *Making journalists: Diverse models, global issues* (pp. 127–56). London: Routledge.

Salwen, M., and Garrison, B. (2013). *Latin American journalism.* 2nd ed. London: Routledge.

Scannell, P. (1989). Public service broadcasting and modern public life. *Media, Culture & Society, 11,* 135–66.

Scheuer, J. (2008). *The big picture: Why democracies need journalistic excellence.* New York: Routledge.

Schifferes, S., Newman, N., Thurman, N., Corney, D., Göker, A., and Martin, C. (2014). Identifying and verifying news through social media. *Digital Journalism, 2,* 406–18.

Schiller, D. (1981). *Objectivity and the news: The public and the rise of commercial journalism.* Philadelphia: Temple University Press.

Schinkel, W., and Noordegraaf, M. (2011). Professionalism as symbolic capital: Materials for a Bourieusian theory of professionalism. *Comparative Sociology, 10*(1), 67–96.

Schlesinger, P. (1999). Changing spaces of political communication: The case of the European Union. *Political Communication, 16*(3), 263–79.

Schramm, W. (1964). *Mass media and national development: The role of information in developing countries.* Stanford: Stanford University Press.

Schudson, M. (1978). *Discovering the news: A social history of American newspapers.* New York: Basic Books.

———. (1993). *Watergate in American memory: How we remember, forget, and reconstruct the past.* New York: Basic Books.

———. (1996a). The politics of narrative form. In M. Schudson, *The power of news* (pp. 53–71). Cambridge, MA: Harvard University Press.

———. (1996b). Question authority: A history of the news interview. In M. Schudson, *The power of news* (pp. 72–93). Cambridge, MA: Harvard University Press.

———. (1998). *The good citizen: A history of American civic life.* New York: Martin Kessler Books.

———. (1999). What public journalism knows about journalism but doesn't know about "public." In T. Glasser (ed.) *The idea of public journalism* (pp. 118–34). New York: Guilford Press.

———. (2001). The objectivity norm in American journalism. *Journalism, 2*(2), 149–70.

———. (2005). The US model of journalism: Exception or exemplar? In H. de Burgh (ed.) *Making journalists: diverse models, global approaches* (pp. 94–106). London: Routledge.

———. (2013). Fourteen or fifteen generations: News as a cultural form and journalism as a historical formation. *American Journalism, 30*(1), 29–35.

Scott, J. W., and Keates, D. (eds.) (2004). *Going public: Feminism and the shifting boundaries of the private sphere.* Urbana: University of Illinois Press.

Searle, J. (1969). *Speech acts: An essay on the philosophy of language.* Cambridge: Cambridge University Press.

Seligman, A. (1992). *The idea of civil society.* Princeton: Princeton University Press.

Seward, R. (2005). Fish or fowl: Kisha clubs and Japanese journalism. *Asia Pacific Media Educator, 16,* 17–26.

Sewell, W. (1992). A theory of structure: duality, agency, and transformation. *The American Journal of Sociology, 98*(1), 1–29.

———. (2005). *Logics of history: Social theory and social transformation.* Chicago: The University of Chicago Press.

Shapiro, I., Brin, C., Bédard-Brûlé, I., and Mychajlowycz, K. (2013). Verification as a strategic ritual. *Journalism Practice, 7,* 657–73.

Shaw, I. S. (2009). Towards an African journalism model: A critical historical perspective. *International Communication Gazette, 71*(6), 491–510.

Shen, F., and Zhang, Z. (2013). Who are the investigative journalists in China?

References

Findings from a survey in 2010. *Chinese Journal of Communication*, 6(3), 374–84.

———. (2014). The identities and demographics of investigative journalists in China. In M. Svensson, E. Saether, and Z. Zhang (eds.) *Chinese investigative journalists' dreams: Autonomy, agency, and voice* (pp. 33–52). Lanham, MD: Lexington Books.

Shibutani, T. (1966). *Improvised news: A sociological study of rumor.* Indianapolis: Bobbs-Merrill.

Shirk, S. (2011). Changing media, changing China. In S. Shirk (ed.) *Changing media, changing China* (pp. 1–36). New York: Oxford University Press.

Shirky, C. (2008). *Here comes everybody: The power of organizing without organizations.* New York: Penguin Press.

Siapera, E., and Veglis, A. (eds.) (2012). *The handbook of global online journalism.* Oxford: Wiley-Blackwell.

Siebert, F. S., Peterson, T. and Schramm, W. (1956). *Four theories of the press: The authoritarian, libertarian, social responsibility, and Soviet communist concepts of what the press should be and do.* Freeport, NY: Books for Libraries Press.

Silverman, C. (2011). Is this the world's best Twitter account? *Columbia Journalism Review*, accessed on October 23, 2015 at: http://www.cjr.org/behind_the_news/is_this_the_worlds_best_twitter_account.php?page=all.

Simon, K. (2013). *Civil society in China: The legal framework from ancient times to the new reform era.* New York: Oxford University Press.

Sims, N. (ed.) (1990). *Literary journalism in the twentieth century.* New York: Oxford University Press.

Singer, J. (2004). More than ink-stained wretches: The resocialization of print journalists in converged newsrooms. *Journalism and Mass Communication Quarterly, 81,* 838–56.

Singer, J. (2005). The political j-blogger: "Normalizing" a new medium form to fill old norms and practics. *Journalism, 6*(2), 173–98.

Singer, J., Hermida, A., Domingo, D., Heinonen, A., Paulussen, S., Quandt, T., Reich, Z., and Vujnovic, M. (2011). *Participatory journalism: Guarding open gates at online newspapers.* Oxford: Blackwell.

Somers, M. (1995). What's political or cultural about political culture and the public sphere toward an historical sociology of concept formation. *Sociological Theory, 13*(2), 113–44.

Sparks, C. (1992). Popular journalism: Theory and practice. In P. Dhalgren and C. Sparks (eds.) *Journalism and popular culture* (pp. 24–44). Newbury Park, CA: Sage.

Sparks, C., and Tulloch, J. (eds.) (2000). *Tabloid tales: Global debates over media standards.* Lanham, MD: Rowman and Littlefield.

Splichal, S. (2001). Imitative revolutions changes in the media and journalism in East-Central Europe. *The Public, 8*(4), 31–58.

References

Stamm, K. R. (1985). *Newspaper use and community ties.* Norwood, NJ: Ablex Publishing Corp.

Starkman, D. (2011). Confidence game: The limited vision of the news gurus. *Columbia Journalism Review,* accessed on October 23, 2015 at: http://www. cjr.org/essay/confidence_game.php.

Starr, P. (2004). *The creation of the media: Political origins of modern communications.* New York: Basic Books.

Steele, J. (2011). Justice and journalism: Islam and journalistic values in Indonesia and Malaysia. *Journalism, 12*(5): 533–49.

Stephens, M. (1988). *A history of news: From the drum to the satellite.* New York: Viking.

Stockmann, D. (2013). *Media commercialization and authoritarian rule in China.* Cambridge: Cambridge University Press.

Streckfuss, R. (1990). Objectivity in journalism: A search and a reassessment. *Journalism Quarterly, 67*(4), 973–83.

Sunstein, C. (1995). *Democracy and the problem of free speech.* New York: The Free Press.

Svennson, M., Saether, E., and Zhang, Z. (eds.) (2014). *Chinese investigative journalists' dreams: Autonomy, agency and voice.* Lanham, MD: Lexington Books.

Swisher, K. (2014). Can print and online content just get along? California Sunday Magazine hopes so. *Re/Code,* accessed on August 23, 2015 at: http:// recode.net/2014/09/15/can-print-and-online-content-just-get-along-california-sunday-magazine-hopes-so/.

Tarde, G. (1901/1969). *Gabriel Tarde on communication and social influence.* T. N. Clark (ed.) Chicago: University of Chicago Press.

Thornton, P., Ocasio, W., and Lounsbury, M. (2012). *The institutional logics perspective: A new approach to culture, structure and process.* New York: Oxford University Press.

Thussu, D. K. (2005). Adapting to globisation: The changing contours of journalism in India. In H. de Burgh (ed.), *Making journalists: Diverse models, global issues* (pp. 127–41). London: Routledge.

Tichenor, P. J., Donohue, G. A., and Olien, C. N. (1980). *Community Conflict and the Press.* Beverly Hills: Sage.

Tilly, C. (1992). *Coercion, capital, and European states, AD 990–1992.* Cambridge, UK: Blackwell.

Tocqueville, de A. (1840/1969). *Democracy in America.* J. P. Mayer (ed.) G. Lawrence (trans.) Garden City, NY: Doubleday and Co.

Todd, C. (1991). *Political bias, censorship, and the dissolution of the "official" press in eighteenth-century France. Studies in French Civilization* (Vol. 8). Lewiston, NY: Edwin Mellen Press.

Tong, J. (2007). Guerrilla tactics of investigative journalism in China. *Journalism, 8*(5), 530–55.

References

Tong, J. (2011). *Investigative journalism in China: Journalism, power, and society*. London: Continuum.

Tong, J., and Sparks, C. (2009). Investigative journalism in China today. *Journalism Studies, 10*(3), 337–52.

Tönnies, F. (1916/2000). *Ferdinand Tönnies on public opinion: Selections and analyses*. H. Hardt and S. Splichal (ed. and trans.) Lanham, MD: Rowman & Littlefield.

———. (1887/1957). *Community and Society*. C. P. Loomis (ed. and trans.) New York: Harper and Row.

Tsui, L. (2003). The panopticon as the antithesis of a space of freedom: Control and regulation of the Internet in China. *China Information, 17*(2), 65–82.

Tuchman, G. (1972). Objectivity as strategic ritual: An examination of newsmen's notions of objectivity. *American Journal of Sociology, 77*(4), 660–79.

———. (1978). *Making news: A study in the construction of reality*. New York: The Free Press.

Turvill, W. (2015). Johnston press closures mean more than 300 UK local newspapers have gone in last ten years. *Press Gazette*, accessed on October 23, 2015 at: http://www.pressgazette.co.uk/johnston-press-closures-mean-more-300–uk-local-newspapers-have-been-closed-ten-years.

Underwood, D. (1993). *When MBAs rule the newsroom*. New York: Columbia University Press.

———. (2013). *The undeclared war between journalism and fiction: Journalists as genre benders in literary history*. New York: Palgrave-Macmillan.

Valeriani, A. (2010). Pan-Arab satellite television and Arab national information systems: Journalists' perspectives on a complicated relationship. *Middle East Journal of Culture and Communication, 3*, 26–42.

van Dijk, J. (2012). *The network society*. 3rd ed. London: Sage.

Vartanova, E. (2012). The Russian media model in the context of post-Soviet dynamics. In D. Hallin and P. Mancini (eds.) *Comparing media systems beyond the Western world* (pp. 119–42). Cambridge: Cambridge University Press.

Voltmer, K. (2008). Comparing media systems in new democracies: East meets South meets West. *Central European Journal of Communication, 1*, 23–40.

Volz, Y. Z., and Lee, C. C. (2009). American pragmatism and Chinese modernization: Importing the Missouri model of journalism education to modern China. *Media, Culture & Society, 31*(5), 711–30.

Waisbord, S. (2000). *Watchdog journalism in South America: News, accountability, and democracy*. New York: Columbia University Press.

———. (2009). Advocacy journalism in a global context. In K. Wahl-Jorgensen, and T. Hanitzsch (eds.) *The handbook of journalism studies* (pp. 371–85). London: Routledge.

———. (2013). *Reinventing professionalism: Journalism and news in a global perspective*. Cambridge, UK: Polity.

References

Waldman, S. (2011). *The information needs of communities: The changing media landscape in a broadband age.* Washington D.C.: Federal Communications Commission.

Ward, S. (2004). *The invention of journalism ethics: The path to objectivity and beyond.* Montreal: McGill-Queen's University Press.

Warner, M. (2002). *Publics and counterpublics.* New York: Zone Books.

Weaver, D. (1998). *The global journalist: News people around the world.* Cresskill, NJ: Hampton Press.

Weaver, D., and Willnat (eds.) (2012). *The global journalist.* New York: Routledge.

Weintraub, J. (1997). The theory and the politics of the public/private distinction. In J. Weintraub (ed.) *Public and private in thought and practice* (pp. 1–42). Chicago: The University of Chicago Press.

Weston, T. B. (2010). China, professional journalism, and liberal internationalism in the era of the First World War. *Pacific Affairs, 83*(2), 327–47.

Wiener, J. H., and Hampton, M. (2007). *Anglo-American media interactions, 1850–2000.* Basingstoke: Palgrave Macmillan.

Wilensky, H. L. (1964). The professionalization of everyone? *The American Journal of Sociology, 70*(2), 137–58.

Williams, R. (1976). *Keywords: A vocabulary of culture and society.* New York: Oxford University Press.

Willig, I. (2012). Newsroom ethnography in a field perspective. *Journalism, 12*(3), 372–87.

Wittgenstein, L. (1958). *Philosophical investigations.* 3rd ed. G. E. M. Anscombe (trans.) New York: Macmillan.

Wolff, M. (2012). Did NPR's Andy Carvin overreach his Twitter calling on Newtown shooting? *The Guardian,* December 17, accessed on October 23, 2015 at http://www.theguardian.com/commentisfree/2012/dec/17/npr-andy-carvin-overreach-newtown.

Xiaoping, L. (2002). "Focus" and the changes in the Chinese television industry. *Journal of Contemporary China, 11*(30), 17–34.

Xiatong, F. (1992). *From the soil: The foundations of Chinese society.* G. Hamilton and Z. Wang (trans. and ed.) Berkeley: University of California Press.

Xin, X. (2012). *How the market is changing China's news: The case of Xinhua news agency.* Lanham, MD: Lexington Books.

Xu, Y., Chu, L. L., and Zhongshi, G. (2002). Reform and challenge: An analysis of China's journalism education under social transition. *International Communication Gazette, 64*(1), 63–77.

Young, I. M. (1990). *Inclusion and democracy.* Oxford: Oxford University Press.

Yuezhi, Z. (2010). Watchdogs or party leashes? Contexts and implications of investigative journalism in post-Deng China. *Journalism Studies, 1*(2), 577–97.

Zaret, D. (2000). *Origins of democratic culture: Printing, petitions, and the*

References

public sphere in early modern England. Princeton, NJ: Princeton University Press.

Zelizer, B. (1990). Achieving journalistic authority through narrative. *Critical Studies in Mass Communication, 7*(4), 366–76.

Zelizer, B. (2012). On the shelf life of democracy in journalism scholarship. *Journalism, 14*(4), 459–73.

Zha, J. (1996). *China pop: How soap operas, tabloids and best sellers are transforming a culture*. New York: The New Press.

Zhang, H., and Su, L. (2012). Chinese media and journalists in transition. In D. Weaver and L. Willnat (eds.) *The global journalist in the 21st century* (pp. 9–21). New York: Routledge.

Zhang, X. (2007). *The origins of the modern Chinese press: The influence of the Protestant missionary press in late Qing China*. London: Routledge.

Zhao, Y. (2000). From commercialization to conglomeration: The transformation of the Chinese press within the orbit of the party state. *Journal of Communication, 50*(2), 3–26.

Zhao, Y. (2004). The state, the market, and media control in China. In P. N. Thomas, and Z. Nain (eds.) *Who owns the media? Global trends and local resistances* (pp. 179–212). London: Zed Books.

Zhao, Y. (2008). *Communication in China: Political economy, power, and conflict*. Lanham, MD: Rowman and Littlefield.

Zhao, Y. (2012). Understanding China's media system in a world historical context. In D. Hallin and P. Mancini (eds.) *Comparing media systems beyond the Western world* (pp. 143–76). Cambridge: Cambridge University Press.

Index

Page numbers in *italics* refer to a figure/table

Index

Index

Index

Index